A Global Security System:
An Alternative to War

2018-19 edition

WORLDBEYONDWAR.org

a global movement to end all wars

SUMMARY

Resting on a convincing body of evidence that violence is not a necessary component of conflict among states and between states and non-state actors, World BEYOND War asserts that war itself can be ended. We humans have lived without war for most of our existence and most people live without war most of the time. Warfare arose about 10,000 years ago (only 5% of our existence as Homo Sapiens) and spawned a vicious cycle as peoples, fearing attack by militarized states, found it necessary to imitate them; and so began the cycle of violence that has culminated in the last 100 years in a condition of permawar. War now threatens to destroy civilization as weapons have become ever more destructive. However, in the last 150 years, revolutionary new knowledge and methods of nonviolent conflict management have been developing that lead us to assert that it is time to end warfare and that we can do so by mobilizing millions around a global effort.

Here you will find the pillars of war which must be taken down so that the whole edifice of the War System can collapse, and here are the foundations of peace, already being laid, on which we will build a world where everyone will be safe. This book presents a comprehensive blueprint for peace as the basis of an action plan to finally end war.

A Global Security System: An Alternative to War (2018-19 Edition)

ISBN: 978-0-9980859-6-8

Produced and published by: World BEYOND War

2018-19 Edition Editor: Tony Jenkins

Original authors: Shifferd, Kent; Hiller, Patrick; Swanson, David

Valuable feedback and/or contributions to this and past editions by: Colin Archer, Steve Bailey, Jim Bearden, Kathy Beckwith, Leah Bolger, Robert Burrowes, Mary DeCamp, Mel Duncan, Pat Elder, Russ Faure-Brac, Ronald Glossop, Judith Hand, David Hartsough, John Horgan, Robert Irwin, Susan Lain Harris, Patricia Mische, Catherine Mullaugh, Margaret Pecoraro, David Prater, Betty Reardon, John Reuwer, Joe Scarry, Annette Schmidt, Alice Slater, Jewell Starsinger, Linda Swanson, Laurie Timmermann, Benjamin Urmston, & Greta Zarro.

Apologies to those who have provided feedback and are not mentioned. Your input is valued.

Layout and design: Paloma Ayala

Contents

HOW THIS BOOK IS ORGANIZED...AND HOW TO USE IT

This book begins with a provocative "Vision of Peace" which may seem to some to be utopian until one reads the rest of the book which comprises the means for achieving it. The first two parts of the book present an analysis of how the current war system works, the desirability and necessity of replacing it, and an analysis of why doing this is possible. The next part outlines the Alternative Global Security System (AGSS) that challenges the failed system of national security and replaces it with the concept of common security - no one is safe until all are safe.

The AGSS relies on three broad strategies for humanity to end war: **1) demilitarizing security, 2) managing conflicts without violence, and 3) creating a culture of peace**. These are the interrelated components of our system: the frameworks, processes, tools and institutions necessary for dismantling the war machine and replacing it with a peace system that will provide a more assured common security. Strategies for demilitarizing security are directed at reducing dependency on militarism. At first glance these strategies seem to be only focused on "undoing" the present system. However, they also establish normative principles for pursuing and achieving security. **Strategies for managing conflict without violence** are focused on reforming and/or establishing new institutions, tools and processes for assuring security. These are the most outwardly functional components of our system. **Strategies for creating a culture of peace** are the most visionary, potentially transformative, and future oriented. These strategies are concerned with establishing social and cultural norms, values, and principles necessary for sustaining a thriving peace system and the means to spread it globally. The remainder of the book addresses realistic steps an individual or group can take, highlighting the efforts of World BEYOND War to accelerate the transition, and ending with a resource guide for further study and action.

This book is an essential learning tool for those curious about and committed to the abolition of war. It is also an invaluable resource for policy recommendations and citizen action for a more peaceful world order. It is designed for personal study, group discussion, and/or classroom use. We encourage you to read it from cover-to-cover, although you may also easily jump in at any point.

AGSS is a dynamic, living resource: while we have documented here significant research and experimentation on alternative approaches to security, and our knowledge and experiences continues to expand rapidly, we are still confronted by a dominating war system. New thinking and knowledge must be continuously developed, so we invite you to treat this as a shared project. As you explore the alternative vision presented here, you are encouraged to formulate your own ideas on the most effective and ethically consistent strategies and institutions as the foundations of a global security system. We also firmly believe that by encouraging learners to formulate their own solutions and map out systems for common security, we are more likely to encourage ownership and political action to bring the new system into being. Citizen action is absolutely essential for the transformation of the present system. So, beyond assessing the alternatives presented, we invite you to consider (and share with us) the actions we might take, as individuals or collectively, to advance possibilities for change.

As noted above, while this book is based on the work of many experts in peace research,

political science, and international relations, as well as on the experience of many activists, it is an evolving plan that will change as we gain more and more experience. The challenges outlined in the first part are real, interconnected, and tremendous. Sometimes we don't make the connections because we don't see them. Sometimes we simply bury our heads in the sand – the problems are too big, too overwhelming, too uncomfortable. The bad news is that the problems won't go away if we ignore them. The good news is that there is reason for authentic hope.[1] The historic end of war is now possible if we muster the will to act and so save ourselves and the planet from ever greater catastrophe. World BEYOND War firmly believes that we can do this.

"Study War No More" – Join Our Online Learning Community

"Study War No More" is our free, online learning guide designed to support further study of this book. Developed in partnership with the Global Campaign for Peace Education, the guide can be used for independent study or as a tool for facilitating dialogue and discussion in classrooms (secondary, university) and with community groups. "Study War No More" presents several discussion topics, each featuring guiding questions to support deeper inquiry of essential topics. "Study War No More" also helps to bring this book to life: each discussion topic includes an introductory video from one of our "study and action partners" – leading global thinkers, strategists, academics, advocates and activists who are already developing components of an alternative global security system. Some of these study and action partners will be introduced throughout this book.

STUDY WAR NO MORE
A Concerned Citizens Study & Action Guide for "A Global Security System: An Alternative to War"

Join "Study War No More," our online learning community here:
www.globalsecurity.worldbeyondwar.org

---

1. Peace activist and professor Jack Nelson-Pallmeyer coined the term "authentic hope" based on the premise that as individuals and collectively we are living in a difficult transition period marked by disruption and discontinuity. This provides us with an opportunity and responsibility to shape the quality of our future. See: Nelson-Pallmeyer, J. (2012). *Authentic hope: It's the end of the world as we know it, but soft landings are possible.* Maryknoll, N.Y.: Orbis Books.

PREFACE TO 2018-19 EDITION

This 4th edition of World BEYOND War's "blueprint for ending war" represents another dynamic evolution in our thinking about what comprises "A Global Security System" and the strategies, new models, and visions necessary for getting us there. This book guides our work and has emboldened members of our community to become active participants and changemakers who are challenging the old system and laying the foundations for the new.

Each year we invite and encourage feedback on "A Global Security System: An Alternative to War" - henceforth AGSS — with the hope and intention of clarifying our vision and making the blueprint easier to follow. Much of our feedback this year came from participants in our intensive online courses, many of whom found it challenging to visualize and articulate the "whole system." The necessary complexity of a systemic framework of this scope can lead to confusion. Thus this edition takes on this call for clarity. Many of the changes you'll find in these pages are structural: some parts have been moved so as to be more logically situated within the framework and a few redundancies have been deleted. Most significant in our attempt at clarity is the addition of a **summary chart outlining the components and strategies of AGSS** as well as a **mind-map / flowchart** that should aid readers in visualizing the interrelationships amongst all the dynamic parts of the system.

New to this edition are short, **executive summaries** to each of the three main components and guiding strategies described in the outline of our system. These summaries help illustrate the strategic balance sought between transitionary reforms to existing security efforts and more transformative proposals advocating for the development of new approaches and institutions. These summaries are also complemented by **strategic policy and action recommendations**. This addition was prompted by a story shared by a community member who had the opportunity to give a copy of AGSS to a U.S. Congresswoman. The Congresswoman's office found AGSS powerful yet too dense for the average lawmaker. These new recommendations distill some of what we believe to be the most critical policy recommendations to be pursued. These recommendations are also focused calls to action: guiding suggestions for political engagement for all concerned.

Another challenge of visualizing AGSS is that many find it difficult to imagine something that has yet to come into being. As with past editions, we share stories of hope and change that illuminate the undocumented and unprecedented peace revolution of modern times; a revolution that is overshadowed by the predominant cultural narrative of militarism. We attempt to breathe a bit more life into these stories by introducing the work of many of our study and action partners: leading global thinkers, strategists, academics, advocates and activists who are already developing components of an Alternative Global Security System. These partners were previously introduced on *Study War No More*, our complementary, free, online learning guide designed to support further study of this book. We share snippets of their stories here with links to video interviews found on *Study War No More*.

The section on "Proposals for Starting Over: Alternative Approaches to Humane Global Governance" has also had a major overhaul. We haven't entirely given up on the United

Nations, but we recognize its many faults, many of which may be too difficult to overcome under the present nation state paradigm. We continue to call for strategic reforms of the current system, but we also believe it's essential to rethink the entire paradigm of global governance. World BEYOND War recently drafted a new framework for a "Global Emergency Assembly (GEA)," a vision for an institution of global governance designed to replace the current UN system. We complement our synopsis of GEA (a work in progress) with a broader introduction to The Earth Federation & The Earth Constitution. These efforts go back to 1958, when the World Constitution and Parliament Association was founded to promote the principles of global democratic governance. We think these proposals represent some of the most promising visions and models for peaceful global governance and share them with the hopes that they will spur much needed new thinking and potentially influence reforms to existing institutions.

As with past editions, we strive to incorporate new and updated data to more accurately illustrate current trends. The contributions from peace research are growing and whenever possible we integrate empirical evidence from analyses in the *Peace Science Digest*[2] to support many of the arguments made. In addition, research institutions like the Stockholm International Peace Research Institute, the Peace Research Institute Oslo, the Institute for Economics and Peace or One Earth Future Research provide data on military spending, business and security, gender and security, peacefulness or lack thereof, and empirically based, actionable strategies and policy recommendations.

We know that we might not sufficiently address all emerging security concerns. For instance, we could easily dedicate an entire volume to address the dilemmas of Trumpism. However, truth-be-told, Donald Trump's escalatory rhetoric hardly represents a new tack in U.S. foreign diplomacy or security policy. While we continue to resist all current and new wars, the mission of World BEYOND War and AGSS is to end all wars - a more long-term, strategic endeavor. We hope this updated edition provides opportunities for new learning, new outreach, and new partnerships that might aid us in moving beyond the choir with our efforts and connect the disconnected. We hope that other movement builders, such as our "study and action partners," will continue to engage in the critical work of building components of the new system as well as identify areas of focus and unity based on developments and insights highlighted in the book.

---

2. https://peacesciencedigest.org/

A GUIDING VISION OF PEACE

There are many different visions of peace, the following is ours. A sustainable future world in which children live free from fear and violence, are nurtured by a culture of peace, and are able to achieve their full human potential is what motivates World BEYOND War's efforts to establish an Alternative Global Security System. This is what we are striving for. The system we establish should be moving us in this direction – if not, we need to reconsider our design. What is your guiding vision of peace? What vision motivates you to take action for change?

"People can't work for what they can't imagine."
Elise Boulding (Founding figure of Peace and Conflict Studies)

We will know we have achieved peace when the world is safe for all children. They will play freely out of doors, never worrying about picking up cluster bombs or about drones buzzing overhead. There will be good education for all children for as far as they are able to go. Schools will be safe and free from fear. The economy will be healthy, producing useful things rather than those things which destroy use value, and producing them in ways that are sustainable. There will be no carbon burning industry, and global warming will have been halted. All children will study peace and will be trained in powerful, peaceful methods of confronting violence, should it arise at all. Children will learn how to defuse and resolve conflicts peacefully. When they grow up they may enlist in a shanti sena, a peace force that will be trained in the unarmed protection of civilians and perfect the use of civilian-based defense, making their nations ungovernable if attacked by another country or a coup d'état and therefore immune from conquest. Children will be healthy because health care will be freely available, funded from the vast sums that once were spent on the war machine. The air and water will be clean, soils healthy and producing healthy food because the funding for ecological restoration will be available from the same source. When we see children playing, we will see children from many different cultures together at their play because restrictive borders will have been abolished. The arts will flourish, and science will focus on constructive rather than destructive ways to create safety and prosperity. While learning to be proud of their own cultures–their religions, arts, foods, traditions, etc.–these children will realize they are citizens of one small planet as well as citizens of their respective countries. They will grow up with respect for democratically agreed-upon international law. These children will never be soldiers, although they may well serve humanity in voluntary organizations or in some kinds of universal service for the common good.

No one is safe until all are safe.

INTRODUCTION: A BLUEPRINT FOR ENDING WAR

"Whatever purpose the war system might once have served, it has now become dysfunctional to future human survival, yet it has not been abolished."
- Patricia M. Mische (Peace Educator)

In *On Violence*, Hannah Arendt wrote that the reason warfare is still with us is not a death wish of our species nor some instinct of aggression, "...but the simple fact that no substitute for this final arbiter in international affairs has yet appeared on the political scene."[1] The Alternative Global Security System we describe here is the substitute: it rejects the failed system of national security and replaces it with the concept of common security - no one is safe until all are safe.

The goal of this book is to gather into one place everything one needs to know to work toward an end to war by replacing it with an Alternative Global Security System – one in which peace is pursued by peaceful means.

The path to ending war and establishing the Alternative Global Security System can be achieved through three broad strategies: 1) demilitarizing security; 2) managing conflicts without violence, and 3) creating a culture of peace. These three strategies are the organizing components of our blueprint.

"What is called national security is a chimerical state of things in which one would keep for oneself alone the power to make war while all other countries would be unable to do so... War is therefore made in order to keep or increase the power of making war."
- Simone Weil (Philosopher and Activist)
cited by Thomas Merton (Catholic Writer)

For nearly all of recorded history we have studied war and how to win it, but war has become ever more destructive and now threatens whole populations and planetary ecosystems with annihilation in a nuclear holocaust. Short of that, it brings "conventional" destruction unimaginable only a generation ago, while looming global economic and environmental crises go unattended. Unwilling to give in to such a negative end to our human story, we have begun to react in positive ways. We have begun to study war with a new purpose: to end it by replacing it with a system of conflict management that will result, at the very least,

---

1. Arendt, H. (1970). *On violence.* New York, NY: Houghton Mifflin Harcourt.

in a minimal peace. This document is a blueprint for ending war. It is not a plan for an ideal utopia. It is a summary of the work of many, based on many years of experience and analysis by people striving to understand why, when almost everyone wants peace, we still have wars; and on the work of countless people who have real-world political experience in nonviolent struggle as a substitute for war.[2] Many of these people have come together to work with World BEYOND War.

THE WORK OF WORLD BEYOND WAR

World BEYOND War is helping build a global nonviolent movement to end war and establish a just and sustainable peace. We believe the time is right for large-scale cooperation among existing civil society organizations seeking peace, justice, human rights, sustainability and other benefits to humanity. We believe that the overwhelming majority of the world's people are sick of war and ready to back a global movement to replace it with a system of conflict management that does not kill masses of people, exhaust resources, and degrade the planet.

World BEYOND War believes that conflict between nations and within nations will always exist and that it is all too frequently militarized with disastrous results for all sides. We believe that humanity can create – and already is in the process of creating – a non-militarized alternative global security system that will resolve and transform conflicts without resort to violence. We also believe that such a system will need to be phased in while phasing out militarized security; hence we advocate such measures as non-provocative defense and international peacekeeping in the early stages of the changeover.

We are confident that viable alternatives to war can and will be constructed. We do not believe we have described a perfect system. This is a work-in-progress that we invite others to improve. Nor do we believe that such an alternative system might not fail in limited ways. However, we are confident that such a system will not fail people in the massive ways that the current war system does, and we also provide means of reconciliation and a return to peace should such limited failures occur.

You will see here the elements of an Alternative Global Security System that does not rely on war or the threat of war. These elements include many for which people have long been working, sometimes for generations: the abolition of nuclear weapons, reform of the United Nations, ending the use of drones, changing national priorities from wars and preparations for war to meeting human and environmental needs, and many others. World BEYOND War intends to cooperate fully with these efforts while mobilizing a mass movement to end war and replace it with an alternative global security system. You can learn more about our current efforts by reading the section *Accelerating the Transition: Building the World BEYOND War Movement*.

---

2. There now exists a large body of scholarship and a wealth of practical experience with creating institutions and techniques to manage conflict and practical experience with successful nonviolent movements, much of which is referenced in the resources section at the end of the A Global Security System: An Alternative to War document and on the World BEYOND War website.

Disclaimer

World BEYOND War is a global movement.

Dismantling the war system and replacing it with an Alternative Global Security System requires us to adopt new thinking that goes beyond borders, and to abandon many of the old mindsets about world order that divide, rather that unite us. We therefore strive in this publication to offer a full integration of international, national, cultural, and gendered understandings and experiences.

We acknowledge that much of the analysis in this book is focused on U.S. military and foreign policy. Of course U.S. militarism is felt throughout the world through military, economic, cultural and political domination. The United States is a big part of the problem, but not the full problem. In our transition to becoming a truly global movement, we seek to bring attention to the pervasiveness of militarism and war in every corner of the planet, as well as integrate more non-Western approaches to peacebuilding and security. We hope that over time this book will reflect a greater diversity of perspectives through our continued effort to seek and integrate your feedback.

It will require a truly global movement to succeed in our mission to abolish war. You are invited to help build this movement.

WHY AN ALTERNATIVE GLOBAL SECURITY SYSTEM IS NECESSARY

Modern history is so vivid in detail about warfare that we tend to assume that war is an attribute of humanity itself. American anthropologist Margaret Mead famously observed that warfare is not in our genes, that it is in fact a human invention. Not only is there no scientific evidence of genetic predispositions to war, there is no viable anthropological evidence[3] to suggest that our hunter gathering ancestors ever engaged in war making activities. In 1986 a group of scientists gathered in Seville, Spain to once and for all put the mythical notion of humanity's innate warlike nature to bed. They produced the Seville Statement on Violence[4] that challenges and refutes the many excuses of biological determinism that are often used to justify going to war.

Margaret Mead argued that war is a culturally learned behavior. She explains this by observing that:

> *"If a people have an idea of going to war and the idea that war is the way in which certain situations, defined within their society, are to be handled, they will sometimes go to war."*
> *- Margaret Mead*

So if war is indeed a human invention, what are we to do about it? War is part of our thoughts and is immortalized in culture through education and military monuments in town squares. Mead argues that other social inventions have faded away, but for this to happen two conditions must be met: 1. We must recognize the defects of the old invention, and 2. we must make a new one to replace it.

Regarding the first condition, we are well aware of the defects of war – indeed, there are no upsides. This introductory section of our blueprint explores these failings.

The second condition is the focus of the rest of the book. With what do we replace the war system? What alternatives current exist that are more preferred than the present? Which must still be imagined? And, once we have a clear vision of a peace system to replace the war system, how might we go about facilitating the transition from the old to the new? What must we know and what skills will we need to build it? What political and practical strategies might we employ? What's our role in this transition?

---

3. While there is some debate on this, there is scant and rapidly disappearing anthropological evidence of lethal group violence prior to 10,000 years ago. See John Horgan - *Survey of Earliest Human Settlements Undermines Claim that War Has Deep Evolutionary Roots:* https://blogs.scientificamerican.com/cross-check/survey-of-earliest-human-settlements-undermines-claim-that-war-has-deep-evolutionary-roots/. **See also Douglas Fry** - *Life Without War:* https://www.academia.edu/18818274/Reprint_Life_without_War

4. Read the *Seville Statement on Violence* here: http://www.culture-of-peace.info/vita/2011/seville2011.pdf

Margaret Mead also alluded to a third condition that must be met for old inventions to fade away: we need to have the belief that social invention is possible.

Getting past the pessimism that the war system imbues within us is no easy task. Futurists are keen to point out that it's difficult to imagine and construct preferred realities when our visions of the future are guided by present probabilities. The present system is so stark that a negative future seems predestined. Such a worldview shapes our thinking about what is possible. We have to shake off the humanly invented chains of the war system and militarism that shape our thinking if we are to move from probably to preferred future realities. In this task its helpful to remember the provocative words of pioneering peace researcher Kenneth Boulding: "Whatever exists is possible." Thinking that war is inevitable makes it so; it's a self-fulfilling prophecy. Thinking that ending war is possible opens the door to constructive work on an actual peace system.

What Makes Us Secure?

Security, particularly national security, unfortunately is defined in relation to military power and its global projection. It is necessary to shift from an anarchic state system security paradigm to one that reflects human and planetary needs. The traditional focus of security thinking has emphasized the nation state and competition for power in the international system.[5] While it is widely recognized that the understanding of security needs to be broadened, immense fiscal resources still are put toward building stronger militaries.

The term "security dilemma" in an anarchic global system of states is described as follows: "According to the security dilemma, actions taken by one state to enhance its security will necessarily decrease the security of other states. By acting to defend itself, a state may inadvertently provoke aggressive reactions from its rivals."[6] The real security dilemma, however, lies at the intersection of an outdated "security through strength" paradigm and a new security paradigm emphasizing human and planetary needs.

The Old Security Paradigm

"The far-flung U.S. military establishment, including hundreds of military bases scattered around the world, will not save civilization. It belongs to another era"
- Lester Brown, Earth Policy Institute

---

5. Kay, S. (2012). *Global security in the twenty-first century: The quest for power and the search for peace (2nd edition).* Lanham, MD: Rowman and Littlefield

6. Levinger, M. B. (2012). *Conflict analysis: Understanding causes, unlocking solutions.* Washington, DC: United States Institute of Peace

The legacy of two world wars and the Cold War in the last century keeps us stuck to defining security almost exclusively through military force.[7] The military security lens is not only visible in "peace through strength" language, but also easily quantifiable in budgetary terms. According to the strongly grounded work of the War Resisters League[8], more than 50% of the federal budget outlays go into the military as opposed to a skewed government depiction of budgetary spending. Basic social services such as education or basic human survival needs such as food security fall short in this picture.

Alternative Security Paradigms

Lester Brown, President of the Earth Policy Institute, recommends a conceptual and fiscal redefinition of security. Climate change, population growth, water shortages, poverty, rising food prices, and failing states are the real security threats as opposed to military forces. While the conceptual change can be understood relatively easily, the vested interests of strong defense industries impede the fiscal implementation. Peace activist Frida Berrigan wrote: "We have to dismantle the military industrial complex and take the profit out of security, catalyze a transformation of thinking so that security means more than bombs and borders and bloodletting, and begin to turn the whole work of the government around so that it serves the needs of people rather than sating the appetites of corporations."[9]

Human Security

Human security is people centered and emphasizes physical safety, economic and social well-being, respect for the dignity and worth of human beings, protection of human rights and fundamental freedoms. Jody Williams, who received the 1997 Nobel Peace Prize for her work to ban landmines, advocates for a human security concept, where peace is defined by human, and not national security, and that it must be achieved through sustainable development, environmental justice and meeting people's basic needs.[10]

Authentic Security

Author and peace studies professor Jack Nelson-Pallmeyer calls for a rejection of American exceptionalism and pretenses to domination in order to unlock our imaginations for pathways to authentic security. Nelson-Pallmeyer goes on to distinguish between authentic security and protection of interests. Authentic security is based on the idea that leaders "take steps to keep families, homes, neighborhoods, and nation safe and secure" (p. 92).

7. Brown, L. (2011). *World on the edge: how to prevent environmental and economic collapse.* New York, NY: W. W. Norton & Company

8. http://www.warresisters.org/pages/piechart.htm

9. http://www.warresisters.org/peaceeconomy

10.2011 **Ted Talk** - http://www.ted.com/talks/jody_williams_a_realistic_vision_for_world_peace.html

Protection of interests, on the other hand, is based on the idea that leaders represent the interests of the wealthy, that our nation has special rights and responsibilities, and that there are many consumptive wants and needs. The second idea is supported by offensive militarism. "Militarism is not defense. Defending interests isn't the same thing as defending legitimate security needs" (p. 94). [11]

Human Needs

John Burton contributed to the field of conflict resolution with his concept based on the human needs theory. His idea was that every person or group has basic needs, and if these needs are not met, the person or group is going to engage in conflict. The five needs are security, participation, autonomy, recognition, and identity. When security is a shared need by all humans, pursuing security through force will not meet everyone's basic human needs.

Alternatives to particular wars are almost never seriously sought and the idea that there might be an alternative to War itself, almost never occurs to people.

Common Security

Conflict management as practiced in the iron cage of war is self-defeating. In what is known as the "security dilemma," states believe they can only make themselves more secure by making their adversaries less secure, leading to escalating arms races that have culminated in conventional, nuclear, biological and chemical weapons of horrific destructiveness. Placing the security of one's adversary in danger has not led to security but to a state of armed suspicion and as a result, when wars have begun, they have been obscenely violent. Common security acknowledges that one nation can only be secure when all nations are. The national security model leads only to mutual insecurity, especially in an era when nation states are porous. The original idea behind national sovereignty was to draw a line around a geographical territory and control everything that attempted to cross that line. In today's technologically advanced world that concept is obsolete. Nations cannot keep out ideas, immigrants, economic forces, disease organisms, information, ballistic missiles, or cyber-attacks on vulnerable infrastructure like banking systems, power plants, and stock exchanges. No nation can go it alone. Security must be global if it is to exist at all.

In its briefest form common security means: **no one is safe until all are safe.**

---

11. Nelson-Pallmeyer, J. (2012). *Authentic hope: it's the end of the World as we know it, but soft landings are possible.* Maryknoll, NY: Orbis Books.

THE IRON CAGE OF WAR: THE PRESENT WAR SYSTEM DESCRIBED

When centralized states began to form in the ancient world, they were faced with a problem we have just begun to solve. If a group of peaceful states were confronted by an armed, aggressive war-making state, they had only three choices: submit, flee, or imitate the war-like state and hope to win in battle. In this way the international community became militarized and has largely remained so. Humanity locked itself inside the iron cage of war. Conflict became militarized. War is the sustained and coordinated combat between groups leading to large numbers of casualties. War also means, as author John Horgan puts it, militarism, the culture of war, the armies, arms, industries, policies, plans, propaganda, prejudices, and rationalizations that make lethal group conflict not only possible but also likely.[12]

Photos: Public Domain / WikiCommons

In the changing nature of warfare, wars are not limited to states. One might speak of hybrid wars, where conventional warfare, terrorist acts, human rights abuses and other forms of large scale indiscriminate violence take place.[13] Non-state actors play an increasingly important role in warfare, which often takes the form of so-called asymmetric warfare.[14]

While particular wars are triggered by local events, they do not "break out" spontaneously. They are the inevitable result of a social system for managing international and civil conflict: the War System. The capacity for war to start at all is reliant upon the War System which prepares the world in advance for particular wars.

---

12. *War Is Our Most Urgent Problem--Let's Solve It* (http://blogs.scientificamerican.com/cross-check/war-is-our-most-urgent-problem-let-8217-s-solve-it/)

13. Read more at: Hoffman, F. G. (2007). *Conflict in the 21st century: the rise of hybrid wars*. Arlington, VA: Potomac Institute for Policy Studies.

14. Asymmetric warfare takes place between fighting parties where relative military power, strategies or tactics differ significantly. Iraq, Syria, and Afghanistan are the best known examples of this phenomenon.

"Military action anywhere increases the threat of military action everywhere."
- Jim Haber (World BEYOND War Steering Committee
Member— 2014-16)

Debunking Myths of War

World BEYOND War's maintains a list of common war myths and the facts that debunk them. See the Appendices for our handout on Debunking Myths of War.

Among common war system myths are:

- War is inevitable; we have always had it and always will.

- War is "human nature."

- War is necessary.

- War is beneficial.

- The world is a "dangerous place."

- The world is a zero-sum game (What you have I can't have and vice versa, and someone will always dominate, better us than "them.")

- We have "enemies."

The War System rests in part on a set of interlocked beliefs and values that have been around so long that their veracity and utility go mostly unquestioned although they are demonstrably false.[15]

"We must abandon unexamined assumptions, e.g., that war will always
exist, that we can continue to wage war and survive, and that we are
separate and not connected."
- Robert Dodge (Board Member, Nuclear Age Peace Foundation)

The War System also includes institutions and weapons technologies. It is deeply embedded in society and its various parts feed into each other so that it is very robust. For example, a handful of wealthy nations produce most of the weaponry used in the world's wars, and justify their own participation in wars on the basis of the damage done by weaponry they have sold or given to poor nations or groups.[16]

---

15. *American wars. Illusions and realities* (2008) by Paul Buchheit clears up 19 misconceptions about U.S. wars and the U.S. war system. David Swanson's *War is a lie* (2016) refutes 14 arguments used to justify wars.

16. For exact data on arms producers by nation, see the 2016 Stockholm International Peace Research Institute Yearbook chapter "Arms Production and Military Services" at https://www.sipri.org/yearbook/2016/14.

Wars are highly organized, preplanned mobilizations of forces prepared long in advance by the War System which permeates all institutions of society. For example, in the United States (a robust example of a war system participant), not only are there war-making institutions such as the executive branch of government where the head of state is also commander in chief, the military organization itself (Army, Navy, Air Force, Marine Corps, Coast Guard) and the CIA, NSA, Homeland Security, and the several War Colleges, but war is also built into the economy, perpetuated culturally in the schools and religious institutions, a tradition carried on in families, glorified at sporting events, made into games and movies, and hyped by the news media. Almost nowhere does one learn of an alternative.

A single small example of just one pillar of the culture's militarism is military recruiting. The U.S. goes to great lengths to enlist young people in the military, calling it "the Service." Recruiters go to great lengths to make "the Service" appear attractive, offering cash and educational inducements and portraying it as exciting and romantic. Never are the downsides portrayed. Recruiting posters do not show maimed and dead soldiers or blasted villages and dead civilians.

In the U.S., the Army Marketing and Research Group National Assets branch maintains a fleet of semi-trailer trucks whose highly sophisticated, attractive, interactive exhibits glorify warfare and are intended for recruiting in "hard to penetrate high schools." The fleet includes the "Army Adventure Semi" and the "All Army Experience" semi and others.[17] Students can play in simulators and fight tank battles or fly Apache attack helicopters and don Army gear for photo ops and get the pitch to join up. The trucks are on the road 230 days per year. The necessity of war is taken for granted and its destructive downside not exhibited. Photojournalist Nina Berman powerfully documented the U.S. Pentagon's self-promotion to the American public beyond the usual TV advertisements and presence at all sorts of sporting events.[18]

Attempting to ascertain the "recruiting budget" is nearly impossible because of the complexity of recruiting today. One would have to request and compile budgetary information on specific programs like the School Recruiting Program, JAMRS,[19] Starbase[20],

---

17. The Mobile Exhibit Company provides "an array of exhibits such as the Multiple Exhibit Vehicles, Interactive Semis, Adventure Semis, and Adventure Trailers manned by Army recruiters in order to re-connect America's People with America's Army and enhance Army awareness among high school and college students and their centers of influence." See the website at: http://www.usarec.army.mil/msbn/Pages/MEC.htm

18. The photo essay can be seen in the story *Guns and Hotdogs How the U.S. Military Promotes its Weapons Arsenal to the Public* at https://theintercept.com/2016/07/03/how-the-us-military-promotes-its-weaponsarsenal-to-the-public/

19. Joint Advertising, Market & Research Studies: http://jamrs.defense.gov/

20. A DOD youth program: http://dodstarbase.org/

JROTC21, ASVAB-CEP22, and DoDSTEM23, along with a hundred other recruiting programs. Many of these expenditures will differ with each branch - and that does not include marketing and Hollywood censorship programs. It is unlikely the DOD knows what it spends on "recruiting."

While wars are often launched or continued without majority public support, wars result in part from a certain, simple mind set. Governments have succeeded in convincing themselves and masses of people that there are only two responses to aggression: submit or fight, be ruled by "those monsters" or bomb them into the Stone Age. Unfortunately, in the 21st century, it has become patently clear that making war does not work to create peace, as the case of the two Gulf Wars, the Afghan War and the Syrian/ISIS war clearly demonstrate. We have entered a state of permawar. Kristin Christman, in *Paradigm for Peace*, suggests by way of analogy an alternative, problem-solving approach to international conflict:

> "We wouldn't kick a car to make it go. If something were wrong with it, we would figure out which system wasn't working and why: How is it not working? Does it turn on a little? Are the wheels spinning in mud? Does the battery need recharging? Are gas and air getting through? Like kicking the car, an approach to conflict that relies on military solutions does not figure things out: It does not distinguish between the causes of violence and does not address aggressive and defensive motivations."[24]

We can end war only if we change the mindset, ask the relevant questions in order to get at the causes of an aggressor's behavior and, above all, see if one's own behavior is one of the causes. Like medicine, treating only the symptoms of a disease will not cure it. In other words, we must reflect before pulling out the gun. This blueprint for peace does that.

The War System does not work. It does not bring peace, or even minimal security. What it produces is mutual insecurity. Yet we go on.

Wars are endemic; in a War System everyone has to beware of everyone else. The world is a dangerous place because the War System makes it so. It is Hobbes's "war of all against all." Nations often believe they are victims of plots and threats by other nations, certain that the others' military might is aimed at their destruction while failing to see their own failings, that their actions are creating the very behavior they fear and arm against as enemies become mirror images of each other. Examples abound: the asymmetrical Arab-Israeli conflict,

21. Junior Reserve Officers' Training Corps: https://en.wikipedia.org/wiki/ Junior_Reserve_Officers%27_ Training_Corps

22. Career exploration program sponsored by the DOD: https://www.asvabprogram.com/

23. DoDSTEM: http://www.dodstem.us/

24. Paradigm for Peace website: https://sites.google.com/site/paradigmforpeace/

the India-Pakistan conflict, the American war on terror that creates ever more terrorists[25]. Each side maneuvers for the strategic high ground. Each side demonizes the other while trumpeting its own unique contribution to civilization. Added to this volatility is the race for minerals, especially oil, as nations pursue an economic model of endless growth and addiction to oil.[26] Further, this situation of perpetual insecurity gives ambitious elites and leaders the opportunity to hold onto political power by fanning popular fears, and it provides tremendous opportunity for profit for arms makers who then support the politicians who fan the flames.[27]

In these ways the War System is self-fueling, self-reinforcing and self-perpetuating. Believing that the world is a dangerous place, nations arm themselves and act belligerently in a conflict, thus proving to other nations that the world is a dangerous place and that therefore they must be armed and act likewise. The goal is to threaten armed violence in a conflict situation in the hopes that it will "deter" the other side, but this fails on a regular basis, and then the goal becomes not to avoid a conflict, but to win it. Alternatives to particular wars are almost never seriously sought and the idea that there might be an alternative to War itself almost never occurs to people. One does not find what one does not seek.

It is no longer sufficient to end a particular war or particular weapons system if we want peace. The entire cultural complex of the War System must be replaced with a different system for managing conflict. Fortunately, as we shall see, such a system is already developing in the real world.

The War System is a choice. The gate to the iron cage is, in fact, open and we can walk out whenever we choose.

*"War, just like deadly diseases, has to be prevented and cured. Violence is
not the right medicine: it does not cure the disease, it kills the patient."*
- Gino Strada, 2015 Right Livelihood Award Recipient

---

25. A 2006 National Intelligence Estimate stated that the war in Iraq has increased the threat of terrorism. The estimate was compiled by 16 intelligence agencies and was the first assessment of global terrorism since the start of the Iraq war. See *Spy Agencies Say Iraq War Worsens Terrorism Threat*: https://www.nytimes.com/2006/09/24/world/middleeast/24terror.html

26. A study found that foreign governments are 100 times more likely to intervene in civil wars when the country at war has large oil reserves. See an analysis and summary of the study in the Peace Science Digest at http://communication.warpreventioninitiative.org/?p=240

27. In-depth sociological and anthropological evidence can be found in these books: 1) Pilisuk, M., & Achord Rountree, J. (2008). *Who benefits from global violence and war: Uncovering a destructive system.* Westport, CT: Praeger Security International. 2) Nordstrom, C. (2004). *Shadows of war: Violence, power, and international profiteering in the twenty-first century.* Oakland, CA: University of California Press.

THE NECESSITY OF AN ALTERNATIVE SYSTEM – WAR FAILS TO BRING PEACE

World War I was justified as the "war to end all war," but war never brings peace. It may bring a temporary truce, a desire for revenge, and a new arms race until the next war.

> *"War is, at first, the hope that one will be better off; next the expectation that the other fellow will be worse off; then the satisfaction that he isn't any better off; and, finally, the surprise at everyone's being worse off."*
> - *Karl Kraus (Writer)*

In conventional terms, the failure rate of war is 50%—that is, one side always loses. But in realistic terms, even the so-called victors take terrible losses.

LOSES OF WAR [28]

War	Casualties
World War II	Total - 50+ million Russia ("victor") - 20 million; U.S. ("victor") - 400,000+
Korean War	South Korea Military - 113,000 South Korea Civilian - 547,000 North Korea Military - 317,000 North Korea Civilian - 1,000,000 China - 460,000 U.S. Military - 33,000+
Vietnam War	South Vietnam Military - 224,000 North Vietnamese Military and Viet Cong - 1,000,000 South Vietnamese Civilians - 1,500,000 North Vietnamese Civilians - 65,000; U.S. Military 58,000+
Iraq (2003-2008)	"Excess" Iraqi Deaths - 1,455,590+ [29] [30] Iraqis Injured – 4,200,000+

28. Number can vary greatly depending on source. The website Death Tolls for the Major Wars and Atrocities of the Twentieth Century (http://necrometrics.com/20c1m.htm) and the Costs of War Project (https://watson.brown.edu/costsofwar) were used to provide much of the data for this table.

29. David Swanson notes that war deaths can very difficult to quantify and are often vastly underreported for propagandistic purposes. "Excess deaths" is a measure referring to deaths exceeding the death rate under pre-war sanctions. For a complete picture of the complexity of these complications see "Ever More Shocked, Never Yet Awed" by David Swanson: http://davidswanson.org/iraq/ . See also "Playing Games with War Deaths" by Nicolas J S Davies: https://consortiumnews.com/2016/01/17/playing-games-with-war-deaths/

30. In 2008 Just Foreign Policy developed a more nuanced and comprehensive formula to calculate approximately 1,455,590 excess deaths from 2003-2008. See an explanation of this formula here: http://www.justforeignpolicy.org/deathcount/explanation

The casualties and victims of war are far more than those killed by direct combat. While there is controversy among those who try to measure war casualties, we warn against underestimating the numbers of civilian casualties as that distracts from the long-lasting human costs of war. We propose that only a more integrative view of war casualties reflects the horrendous consequences. A thorough war casualty assessment must include direct and indirect war deaths. Indirect victims of war can be traced back to the following:

- Destruction of infrastructure

- Landmines

- Use of depleted uranium

- Refugees and internally displaced people

- Malnutrition

- Diseases

- Lawlessness

- Intra-state killings

- Victims of rape and other forms of sexual violence

- Social injustice

- Lives that could have been saved by redirected spending

- Environmental devastation

War also victimizes in many other ways beyond killing. In June 2016, the United Nations High Commission on Refugees (UNHCR) stated that "wars and persecution have driven more people from their homes than at any time since UNHCR records began." 44,400 people a day are forced to flee their homes because of conflict and persecution. A total of 68.5 million people were forcibly displaced in 2017.[31] Some 4.5 million Iraqis have become refugees since 2003, roughly half of them outside the nation of Iraq. Roughly half of the refugees are children.[32] We also must consider other indirect losses including property, means of employment, interrupted education, broken families, environmental devastation, and a host of others. Only by considering such "indirect" war casualties and victims, can the myth of "clean," "surgical" warfare, with declining numbers of combat casualties, be rightfully countered.

"The havoc wreaked upon civilians is unparalleled, intended and unmitigated."
- Kathy Kelly, Peace Activist

---

31. See Global Trends. Forced Displacement in 2017 (http://www.unhcr.org/globaltrends2017/)

32. See *REFUGEES: How Many People Has the United States Driven from Their Homes in Iraq?* (http://davidswanson.org/iraq/)

Furthermore, in the late twentieth and early twenty-first centuries, wars seem not to end, but to drag on without resolution for years and even decades without peace ever being achieved. Wars do not work. They create a state of perpetual war, or what some analysts are now calling "permawar." In the last 120 years the world has suffered many wars as the following partial list indicates:

The Spanish American War, the Balkan Wars, World War One, the Russian Civil War, the Spanish Civil War, World War Two, the Korean War, the Vietnam War, wars in Central America, the Wars of the Yugoslav Devolution, the First and Second Congo Wars, Iran-Iraq War, the Gulf Wars, the Soviet and U.S. Afghanistan wars, the US Iraq war, the Syrian War, and various others including Japan versus China in 1937, long civil war in Colombia (ended in 2016), and wars in the Sudan, Ethiopia and Eritrea, the Arab-Israeli wars (a series of military conflicts between Israeli and various Arab forces), Pakistan versus India, etc.

WAR IS BECOMING EVER MORE DESTRUCTIVE

The costs of war are immense on a human, social, economic and environmental level. Ten million died in World War I, 50 to 100 million in World War II. The war begun in 2003 killed 5 percent of the people in Iraq.[33] Nuclear weapons could, if used, end human societies or even life on the planet. In modern wars it is not only soldiers that die on the battlefield. The concept of "total war" carries the destruction to non-combatants as well so that today many more civilians— women, children, old men—die in wars than do soldiers. It has become a common practice of modern armies to indiscriminately rain high explosives on cities where large concentrations of civilians try to survive the carnage.

"As long as war is looked upon as wicked, it will always have its fascination.
When it is looked upon as vulgar, it will cease to be popular."
- Oscar Wilde (Writer and Poet)

In 2017, violence cost the world $ 14.76 trillion or $1.988 per person, globally. This measure provided by the Institute of Economics and Peace (IEP) in their 2018 Global Peace Index proves that economic losses dwarf the expenditures and investments in peacebuilding and peacekeeping.[34]

---

33. See more at: http://davidswanson.org/iraq

34. See 2018 Global Peace Index Report at http://visionofhumanity.org/indexes/global-peace-index/

According to Mel Duncan, co-founder of the Nonviolent Peaceforce, the cost for a professional and paid unarmed civilian peacekeeper is $50,000 per year, compared to the $1 million it costs U.S. taxpayers for a soldier in Afghanistan per year.[35]

War Preparation and War are Major Contributors to the Environmental Crisis

Photo: Burning oilfield during Operation Desert Storm, Kuwait. (Photo by Jonas Jordan, United States Army Corps of Engineers via Wikimedia Commons [public domain]) https://commons.wikimedia.org/wiki/File:Kuwait_burn_oilfield.png

In the whole of human history there has been no era of greater environmental destruction than the present. Scientists are speaking out about the danger of undermining the life support system on which civilization depends, and the situation is worsening.[36] We are in the midst of the greatest extinction crisis in 60 million years, unweaving the web of life by massive habitat destruction, as well as toxification from 80,000 man-made chemicals for which nature has no evolutionary experience. We are in the midst of a rapidly accelerating warming of the planet due to the exponential growth of fossil fuel emissions over the last hundred and fifty years. The consequences are already being felt in deadly heat waves that have killed thousands, more frequent and severe storms that bring billions of dollars of

35. The estimated costs of soldier per year in Afghanistan range from $ 850,000 to $ 2.1 million depending on the source and year. See for example the report by the Center for Strategic and Budgetary Assessments at http://csbaonline.org/wp-content/uploads/2013/10/Analysis-of-the-FY-2014-Defense-Budget.pdf or the report by the Pentagon comptroller at http://security.blogs.cnn.com/2012/02/28/one-soldier-one-year-850000-and-rising/. Regardless of the exact number, it is clear that it is exorbitant.

36. We recommend *The War and Environment Reader* (2017) edited by Gar Smith for a thorough historical analysis of the damage military violence inflicts on regional—and global—ecosystems. http://justworldbooks.com/books/war-environment-reader/

property damage, rising sea levels that are already sending refugees toward higher ground and which will eventually send millions seeking asylum in other countries, exacerbating conflict at the borders. Then there are melting glaciers that feed the great irrigation rivers of India and Southwest Asia, causing extreme floods and, when they dry up, severe agricultural losses leading to food shortages as the population nevertheless continues to grow. Deserts are expanding and moving north, also impacting agriculture and forestry, as are disease organisms and parasites. And the CO_2 from burning fossil fuels and from deforestation is acidifying the oceans and imperiling the bottom of the food chain on which millions rely for protein. Elsewhere are vast dead zones in the ocean, deprived of oxygen as a result of fertilizer runoff. And this is only a short list.

Climate change, environmental degradation and resource scarcity are contributing factors to war and violence, often increasing the likelihood of human conflict.[37] Some talk about a catastrophic convergence of poverty, violence, biotic simplification and climate change. While we should not isolate those factors as causal drivers of war, they need to be understood as additional - and probably increasingly important - elements that are part of the social, political, and historical context of a war system.

Military activity, whether preparing for war or actually fighting it, accelerates these life-threatening trends.[38] For example:

- Military aircraft consume about one quarter of the world's jet fuel

- The U.S. Department of Defense uses more fuel per day than the country of Sweden

- An F-16 fighter bomber consumes almost twice as much fuel in one hour as a high-consuming us motorist burns a year

- The U.S. military uses enough fuel in one year to run the entire mass transit system of the nation for 22 years

- One military estimate in 2003 was that two-thirds of the U.S. Army's fuel consumption occurred in vehicles that were delivering fuel to the battlefield

- The military contributes to toxifying our environment

- The U.S. Department of Defense generates more chemical waste than the five largest chemical companies combined

- The majority of the Superfund sites in the U.S. are on military bases

- During the 1991 aerial campaign over Iraq, the U.S. utilized approximately 340 tons of missiles containing depleted uranium (DU) — there were significantly higher rates of cancer, birth defects and infant mortality in Fallujah, Iraq in early 2010

---

37. Michael Klare's *Resource wars: The new landscape of global conflict* (2001) is a good primer on this topic.

38. World BEYOND War's #NoWar2017 conference explored the theme of "War and the Environment." You can find resources, videos and other documentation supporting many of the claims in this section via the #NoWar2017 conference website: https://worldbeyondwar.org/nowar2017/. Additional supporting references and resources can be found here: https://worldbeyondwar.org/war-threatens-environment-resources/

Preparations for war degrade and destroy the ecosystems upon which civilization rests. Most Superfund sites[39] in the U.S. are on military bases. Nuclear weapons factories like Fernald in Ohio and Hanford in Washington State have contaminated ground and water with radioactive waste that will be poisonous for thousands of years. Practicing for warfare, especially artillery practice and bombing runs (which number in the thousands each year), endanger wildlife by killing animals outright, destroying habitat, and creating stress from noise and explosions. The U.S. Navy's testing of its worldwide underwater sonar system involves powerful explosions that derange whales and other sea creatures, damaging their hearing and their own biological sonar systems. War fighting leaves thousands of square miles of land useless and dangerous because of landmines, depleted uranium weapons, and bomb craters that fill with water and become malaria infested. Chemical weapons destroy rainforest and mangrove swamps.

The militaries of the world, and especially of the U.S., deprive nations of acutely needed resources to deal with climate mitigation, rebuilding damaged infrastructure, and ecological restoration. Hundreds of billions of dollars go into destroying things of value rather than creating useful things. Finally, all the wars and threats of war distract us from the crucial task of protecting the environment upon which our generation, and future generations, depend.

"What is happening with climate change, and it is becoming increasingly visible, is that its natural effects make the human habitat less secure in various places."
- Dan Smith, Director Stockholm International Peace Research Institute

Climate change matters for peace and security. Climate factors are already adding dimensions to social conflicts such as in Somalia, Darfur or Mali. The Stockholm International Peace Research Institute (SIPRI) makes it clear that these risks are not future hypothetical ones, but clear, proven and current ones. The broad categories of risk, according to SIPRI, are livelihood conditions, critical infrastructure and migration.

If we do not end war and turn our attention to the planetary crisis, the world we know will end in another and more violent Dark Age.

THE BENEFITS OF AN ALTERNATIVE SYSTEM

The benefits are: no more mass killing and maiming, no more living in fear, no more grief from losing loved ones in wars, no more trillions of dollars wasted on destruction and preparing for destruction, no more pollution and environmental destruction that comes from

---

39. Superfund sites are EPA designated locations where extreme hazardous waste threatens human health and the environment. You can search for Superfund sites via the EPA website: https://www.epa.gov/ superfund/search-superfund-sites-where-you-live. See here for a short-list of military Superfund sites: https:// en.wikipedia.org/wiki/Category:Military_Superfund_sites

wars and preparing for wars, no more war-driven refugees and war-induced humanitarian crises, no more erosion of democracy and civil liberties as government centralization and secrecy are rationalized by a war culture, no more maiming and dying from weapons left over from long-ago wars.

The Institute for Economics and Peace, the National Priorities Project, Costs of War, the War Resisters League, the Stockholm International Peace Research Institute and others are doing invaluable work regarding the absurd burden of war costs on the public.

"The overwhelming majority of people from all cultures prefer to live in peace. At the deepest level of our being, people hate war. Whatever our culture, we share a desire for the good life, which most of us define as having a family, raising children and watching them grow into successful adults, and doing the work that we find meaningful. And war grotesquely interferes with those desires."
- Judith Hand (Author)

WHY WE THINK A PEACE SYSTEM IS POSSIBLE

Thinking that war is inevitable makes it so; it's a self-fulfilling prophecy. Thinking that ending war is possible opens the door to constructive work on an actual peace system.

THERE IS ALREADY MORE PEACE IN THE WORLD THAN WAR

The twentieth century was a time of monstrous wars, yet most nations did not fight other nations most of the time. The U.S. fought Germany for six years, but was at peace with the country for ninety-four years; the war with Japan lasted four years, the two countries were at peace for ninety-six.[40] The U.S. has not fought Canada since 1815, and has never fought Sweden or India. Guatemala has never fought France. The truth is that most of the world lives without war most of the time. In fact, since 1993, the incidence of interstate warfare has been declining.[41] At the same time, we acknowledge the changing nature of warfare as discussed previously. This is most notable in the vulnerability of civilians. In fact, the purported protection of civilians has been increasingly used as a justification for military interventions (e.g. the 2011 overthrow of the government of Libya).

WE HAVE CHANGED MAJOR SYSTEMS IN THE PAST

Largely unanticipated change has happened in world history many times before. The ancient institution of slavery was largely abolished within less than a hundred years — though significant new types of slavery can be found hiding in various corners of the earth, it is illegal and universally considered reprehensible. In the West, the status of women has improved dramatically in the last hundred years. In the 1950s and 1960s over a hundred nations freed themselves from colonial rule that had lasted centuries. In 1964 legal segregation was overturned in the U.S. In 1993, European nations created the European Union after fighting each other for over a thousand years. Disagreements like Greece's recent debt crisis or the 2016 Brexit vote - Britain leaving the European Union - are dealt with through social and political means, not through warfare. Some changes have been wholly unanticipated and have come so suddenly as to be a surprise even to the experts, including the 1989 collapse of the Eastern European communist dictatorships, followed in 1991 by the collapse of the Soviet Union. In 1994 we saw the end of apartheid in South Africa. 2011 saw the "Arab Spring" uprising for democracy catch most experts by surprise.

---

40. The U.S. has 174 bases in Germany and 113 in Japan (2015). These bases are widely considered "remnants" of World War II, but are what David Vine examines in his book *Base Nation*, showing the global base network of the U.S. as a questionable military strategy.

41. A comprehensive work on the decline of warfare: Goldstein, J. S. (2011). *Winning the war on war: The decline of armed conflict worldwide.* New York, NY: Dutton/Penguin.

WE LIVE IN A RAPIDLY CHANGING WORLD

The degree and pace of change in the last hundred and thirty years is hard to comprehend. Someone born in 1884, potentially the grandparent of people now alive, was born before the automobile, electric lights, radio, the airplane, television, nuclear weapons, the internet, cell phones, and drones, etc. Only a billion people lived on the planet then. They were born before the invention of total war. And we are facing even greater changes in the near future. We are approaching a population of nine billion by 2050, the necessity of ceasing to burn fossil fuels, and a rapidly accelerating climate shift that will raise sea levels and flood coastal cities and low-lying areas where millions live, setting in motion migrations the size of which has not been seen since the fall of the Roman Empire. Agricultural patterns will change, species will be stressed, forest fires will be more common and widespread, and storms more intense. Disease patterns will change. Water shortages will cause conflicts. We cannot continue to add in warfare to this pattern of disorder. Furthermore, in order to mitigate and adapt to the negative impacts of these changes we will need to find huge resources, and these can effectively come from appropriating the military budgets of the world, which today amount to two trillion dollars a year.

As a result, conventional assumptions about the future will no longer hold. Very large changes in our social and economic structure are beginning to occur, whether by choice, by circumstances we have created, or by forces that are out of our control. This time of great uncertainty has huge implications for the mission, structure and operation of military systems. However, what is clear is that military solutions are not likely to work well in the future. War as we have known it is fundamentally obsolete.

THE PERILS OF PATRIARCHY ARE BEING CHALLENGED

Sociologists, feminist scholars and peace researchers[42] identify patriarchy as a mindset and system of social organization that privileges certain masculine ways of conducting politics, structuring laws, and shaping the economic, ecological and social relations that guide our lives. Patriarchy is rooted in the social construct of gender, "the culturally defined and socially sanctioned roles in human affairs played by men and women and the characteristics attributed to each that have rationalized these roles."[43]

Patriarchy is associated with social values culturally defined as masculine, including dependence on hierarchy, control, authoritarianism, autonomy, separation, exclusion, and

---

42. The scholarship of Gerda Lerner, Betty Reardon and Elise Boulding are particularly formative to the articulation and observation of patriarchy. See: 1) Lerner, G. (1986). *The creation of patriarchy*. New York, NY: Oxford University Press. 2) Reardon, B. (1995). *Sexism and the war system*. New York, NY: Syracuse University Press. 3) Boulding, E. (1976). *The underside of history*. Boulder, CO: Westview Press.

43. Jenkins, T & Reardon, B. (2007). Gender and Peace: Towards an Gender Inclusive, Holistic Perspective. In Galtung, J. and Webel, C. (Eds.), *Handbook of peace and conflict studies*. New York, NY: Routledge.

competition. Many feminist political scholars[44] have observed that men's historical dominion over the public domain has shaped a social, economic[45] and political order dominated by these traits. War, militarization and militarism represent the pinnacle of negative patriarchal values, thinking and behavior.[46] Feminist peace scholar Betty Reardon observed the strong linkage between sexism[47] and militarism and argued that you can't eliminate violence against women[48] without abolishing war and eliminating militarism and the thinking and values it brings to society. The masculine bias in security decision-making and practice limits diverse perspective considerations and narrows the repertoire of conflict resolution strategies that might be used.

Feminist peace researchers are challenging the patriarchal paradigm by introducing feminist perspectives on security. These perspectives are more closely linked to human security[49], where interdependence, care, human rights, basic needs and relationships are fundamental considerations. The feminist approach also takes into account the day-to-day lived reality of those impacted by violence and focuses on the more subjective private realities of human existence. Reardon argues that authentic change can only emerge from the integration of masculine and feminine perspectives, modes of thought, and processes for designing new systems and the education necessary to achieve them. This is the intention behind many of the political strategies called forth within the UN system that mandate the inclusion of a gender perspective in security decision making and peacebuilding (see the component of our security system addressing "The Role of Women in Peace and Security" for a full articulation of these strategies).

Patriarchy is so imbued into our system of security that it appears to be natural. The good news is that gender is a social construct – it is not biologically determined. Gender roles

---

44. To name a few: Elise Boulding, Cynthia Enloe, Gerda Lerner, Betty Reardon, J. Anne Tickener, & Marilyn Waring. See all footnotes in this section.

45. See especially the work of Marilyn Waring: Waring, M. (1988). *Counting for nothing*. Wellington, New Zealand: Bridget Williams Books Limited.

46. The work of feminist international relations and security scholars Cynthia Enloe, J. Anne Tickner and Cynthia Cockburn has helped illustrate the connection between gender and security. See especially, 1) Enloe, C. (1989). *Bananas, beaches, and bases: Making feminist sense of international relations*. Berkeley: University of California Press; 2) Enloe, C. (2000). *Maneuvers: The international politics of militarizing women's lives*. Berkeley: University of California Press; 3) Cockburn, C. (1998). *The space between us: Negotiating gender and national identities in conflict*. London: Zed Books; and 4) Tickner, J.A. (1992). *Gender in international relations*. New York, NY: Columbia University Press.

47. Sexism can be understood as prejudice or discrimination based on sex or gender.

48. Reardon and colleagues argue that violence against women is integral to war and armed conflict and have identified the many forms of military violence against women (MVAW) and their functions in warfare. For a comprehensive list of forms of MVAW and recommendations for addressing these, see "Violence against Women is Integral to War and Armed Conflict – The Urgent Necessity of the Universal Implementation of UNSCR 1325" at: https://www.i-i-p-e.org/projects/mvaw/

49. The concept "human security" was first articulated by feminist peace scholars long before it was mainstreamed into UN discourse.

and expectations are fluid and dynamic, varying across cultures and changing over time. Critical examination of gendered stereotypes has led to replacing outdated biases with more nuanced thinking. The binary gender categories of our past are beginning to blur. If an era of enlightenment is at hand, we must be willing to alter our attitudes. More fluid gender identities are emerging, and that is a positive step.

Recent research has shown that greater gender equity in politics and business within a state is equated with lower rates of direct violence. Consequently, a larger gender gap is a good predictor of a state's propensity to engage in violent conflict.[50]

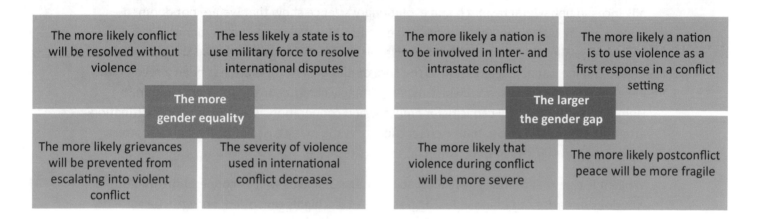

Many other positive trends are showing that patriarchy can be successfully challenged. Micro-loans are empowering women in countries with histories of misogyny. Educating girls is correlated with lowering birth rates and raising standards of living. Female genital mutilation is being discussed and challenged in areas of the globe where male control has always been the standard operating procedure. Women are playing greater roles in designing peacebuilding processes. And, as of January of 2018 full gender parity was achieved in the upper levels of leadership within the United Nations for the first time. Twenty-three of the forty-four members of the Secretary General's Senior Management Group are now women. This follows the precedent set by Canada's Prime Minister, Justin Trudeau, in his choosing to govern with a gender-balanced cabinet. We should consider

50. See: Crespo-Sancho, C. (2017). "The Role of Gender in the Prevention of Violent Conflict." Background paper for the United Nations-World Bank Flagship Study, *Pathways for Peace: Inclusive Approaches to Preventing Violent Conflict*. World Bank, Washington, DC. http://blogs.worldbank.org/dev4peace/can-gender-equality-prevent-violent-conflict

mandating, internationally, in all governments, the same parity not only for all elected offices but all civil servant positions. The progress on women's rights is substantial; achieving full equality with males will yield healthier, happier, and more robust societies.

COMPASSION AND COOPERATION ARE PART OF THE HUMAN CONDITION

The bottom line is that cooperation and compassion are as much a part of the human condition as violence.

The War System is based on the false belief that competition and violence are the result of evolutionary adaptations, a misunderstanding of a popularization of Darwin in the nineteenth century that pictured nature as "red in tooth and claw" and human society as a competitive, zero-sum game where "success" went to the most aggressive and violent. But advances in behavioral research and evolutionary science show that we are not doomed to violence by our genes, that sharing and empathy also have a solid evolutionary basis. Since the Seville Statement on Violence was released in 1986, which refuted the notion of innate and inescapable aggression as the core of human nature, there has been a revolution in behavioral science research which overwhelmingly confirms that earlier declaration.[51] Humans have a powerful capacity for empathy and cooperation, which military indoctrination attempts to blunt with less-than-perfect success as the many cases of post-traumatic stress syndrome and suicides among returning soldiers testify.

While it is true that humans have a capacity for aggression as well as cooperation, modern war does not arise out of individual aggression—it is a highly organized, and structured form of learned behavior that requires governments to plan for it ahead of time and to mobilize the whole society in order to carry it out. The bottom line is that cooperation and compassion are as much a part of the human condition as is violence. We have the capacity for both and the ability to choose either, but while making this choice on an individual, psychological basis is important, it must lead to a change in social structures.

"War does not go forever backwards in time. It had a beginning. We are not wired for war. We learn it."
- Brian Ferguson (Professor of Anthropology)

---

51. The Seville Statement on Violence was designed by a group of leading behavioral scientists to refute "the notion that organized human violence is biologically determined". The entire statement can be read here: http://www.unesco.org/cpp/uk/declarations/seville.pdf

A Global Security System: An Alternative to War 2018-19 Edition

THE IMPORTANCE OF STRUCTURES OF WAR AND PEACE

It is not enough for the world's people to want peace. Most people do, but nonetheless support a war when their nation state or ethnic group calls for it. Even passing laws against war, such as the creation of the League of Nations in 1920 or the famous Kellogg-Briand Pact of 1928 which outlawed war and was signed by the major nations of the world and never formally repudiated, were always understood by their creators as components of necessarily broader systemic changes needed to end war.[52] Both of these laudable moves were created within a robust War System and by themselves could not prevent further wars. Creating the League and outlawing war were necessary but not sufficient. What is sufficient is to create a robust structure of social, legal and political systems that will achieve and maintain an end to war. The War System is made up of such interlocked structures which make war normative. Therefore, an Alternative Global Security System to replace it must be designed in the same way. Fortunately, such a system has been developing for over a century.

> *"Almost nobody wants war. Almost everybody supports it. Why?"*
> *- Kent Shifferd (Author, Historian)*

AN ALTERNATIVE SYSTEM IS ALREADY DEVELOPING

As previously mentioned, evidence from archeology and anthropology now indicate that warfare was a social invention about 10,000 years ago with the rise of the centralized state, slavery and patriarchy. We learned to do war. Yet, for over a hundred thousand years prior, humans lived without large-scale violence. The War System has dominated some human societies since about 4,000 B.C. Beginning in 1816, with the creation of the first citizen-based organizations working to end war, a string of revolutionary developments has occurred. We are not starting from scratch. While the twentieth century was the bloodiest on record, it will surprise most people that it was also a time of great progress in the development of the structures, values, and techniques that will, with further development pushed by nonviolent people power, become an Alternative Global Security System. These are revolutionary developments unprecedented in the thousands of years in which the War System has been the only means of conflict management. Today a competing system exists—embryonic, perhaps, but developing. Peace is real.

By the mid-nineteenth century the desire for international peace was developing rapidly. As a result, in 1899, for the first time in history, an institution was created to deal with global-level conflict. Popularly known as the World Court, the International Court of Justice exists to adjudicate interstate conflict. Other institutions followed rapidly including the first effort at a

---

52. In *The internationalists: How a radical plan to outlaw war remade the* world (2017) by Oona Hathaway and Scott Shapiro and *When the world outlawed war* (2011) by David Swanson, the authors show how people around the world worked to abolish war, outlawing war with a treaty that is still on the books.

world parliament to deal with interstate conflict, the League of Nations. In 1945 the UN was founded, and in 1948 the Universal Declaration of Human Rights was signed. In the 1960s, two nuclear weapons treaties were signed – the Partial Test Ban Treaty in 1963 and the Nuclear Non-Proliferation Treaty which was opened for signature in 1968 and went into force in 1970. More recently, the Comprehensive Test Ban Treaty in 1996[53], the landmines treaty (Antipersonnel Landmines Convention) in 1997, and in 2014 the Arms Trade Treaty were adopted.[54] The landmine treaty was negotiated through unprecedented successful citizen-diplomacy in the so-called "Ottawa Process," where NGOs, together with governments, negotiated and drafted the treaty for others to sign and ratify. The Nobel Committee recognized the efforts by International Campaign to Ban Landmines (ICBL) as a "convincing example of an effective policy for peace" and awarded the Nobel Peace Prize to ICBL and its coordinator Jody Williams.[55] The International Criminal Court was established in 1998 and entered into force in 2002. Laws against the use of child soldiers have been agreed on in recent decades.

NONVIOLENCE: THE FOUNDATION OF PEACE

As these were developing, Mahatma Gandhi and then Martin Luther King Jr., and others, developed a powerful means of resisting violence, the method of nonviolence, now tested and found successful in many conflicts in different cultures around the world. Nonviolent struggle changes the power relationship between oppressed and oppressor. It reverses seemingly unequal relationships, as for example in the case of the "mere" shipyard workers and the Red Army in Poland in the 1980s (the Solidarity Movement led by Lech Walesa ended the repressive regime—Walesa ended up as president of a free and democratic Poland), and in many other cases. Even in the face of the what is considered one of the most dictatorial and evil regimes in history – the German Nazi regime – nonviolence has shown successes on different levels. For example, in 1943, Christian German wives launched a nonviolent protest until almost 1,800 imprisoned Jewish husbands were released. This campaign now is commonly known as the Rosenstrasse Protest. On a larger scale, the Danes launched a 5-year campaign of nonviolent resistance to refuse to assist the Nazi war machine that saved Danish Jews from being sent to concentration camps.[56]

---

53. The Comprehensive Ban Treaty never entered into force as a number of required nuclear weapons states have either not signed, or have signed and not yet ratified the treaty. (https://www.un.org/disarmament/wmd/nuclear/ctbt/)

54. See more on the Arms Trade Treaty in the section: "Outlaw the Arms Trade"

55. See more on the ICBL and citizen diplomacy in *Banning landmines: Disarmament, citizen diplomacy, and human security* (2008) by Jody Williams, Stephen Goose, and Mary Wareham.

56. This case is well documented in the Global Nonviolent Action Database (http://nvdatabase.swarthmore.edu/content/danish-citizens-resist-nazis-1940-1945) and the documentary series A Force More Powerful (www.aforcemorepowerful.org/).

Nonviolence scholar Gene Sharp's consent theory of power illuminates that all government power rests on the consent of the governed and that consent can always be withdrawn.[57] Herein lies the true power of nonviolence. As we shall see, it changes the social psychology of the conflict situation and thus erodes the will of the oppressor to continue injustice and exploitation. It renders oppressive governments helpless and makes the people ungovernable. There are many modern instances of the successful use of nonviolence. Gene Sharp writes: "A vast history exists of people who, refusing to be convinced that the apparent 'powers that be' were omnipotent, defied and resisted powerful rulers, foreign conquerors, domestic tyrants, oppressive systems, internal usurpers and economic masters. Contrary to usual perceptions, these means of struggle by protest, noncooperation and disruptive intervention have played major historical roles in all parts of the world."[58]

Erica Chenoweth and Maria Stephan have demonstrated statistically that, from 1900 to 2006, nonviolent resistance was twice as successful as armed resistance and resulted in more stable democracies with less chance of reverting to civil and international violence. In short, nonviolence works better than war.[59] Chenoweth was named one of the 100 Top Global Thinkers by Foreign Policy in 2013 "for proving Gandhi right." We also know now that countries are more likely to experience the onset of nonviolent campaigns when there is a greater amount of mobilization globally - nonviolence is contagious![60]

---

57. Sharp, G. (1973). *The politics of nonviolent action.* Boston, MA: Porter Sargent

58. Sharp, G. (1980). *Making the abolition of war a realistic goal.* Cambridge, MA: The Albert Einstein Institution. Available at: https://www.aeinstein.org/wp-content/uploads/2013/09/MakingtheAbolitionofWaraRealisticGoal-English.pdf

59. Chenoweth, E, & Stephan, M. (2011). *Why civil resistance works: The strategic logic of nonviolent conflict.* New York, NY: Columbia University Press

60. "Contagious Nonviolence": http://communication.warpreventioninitiative.org/contagious-nonviolence/

Nonviolence is a practical alternative. Nonviolent resistance, coupled with strengthened institutions of peace, now allows us to escape from the iron cage of warfare into which we trapped ourselves six thousand years ago.

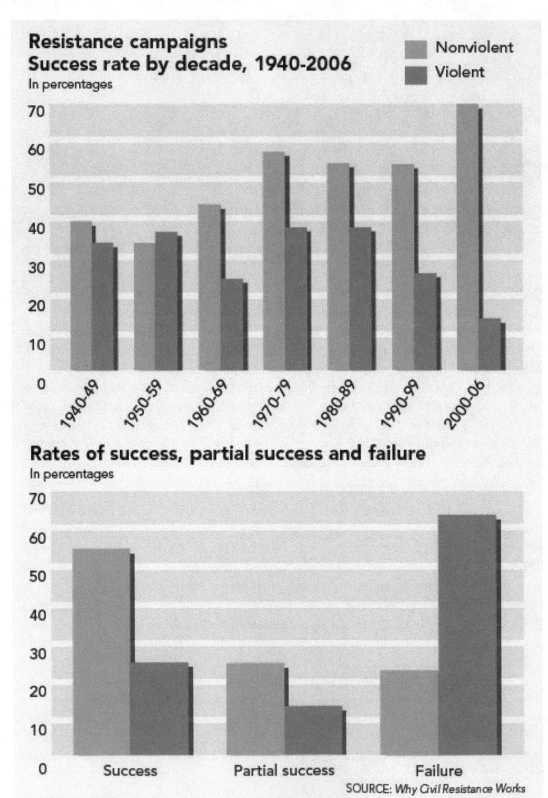

**Resistance campaigns
Success rate by decade, 1940-2006**
In percentages

Nonviolent
Violent

Rates of success, partial success and failure
In percentages

SOURCE: *Why Civil Resistance Works*

Other cultural developments have also contributed toward building a peace system including the powerful movement for women's rights (including educating girls), and the appearance of tens of thousands of citizen groups dedicated to working for international peace, disarmament, strengthening international peacemaking, and peacekeeping institutions. These NGOs are driving this evolution toward peace. Here we can mention only a few such as the Fellowship of Reconciliation, Women's International League for Peace and Freedom, the American Friends Service Committee, the United Nations Association, Veterans For Peace, the International Campaign to Abolish Nuclear Weapons, The Hague Appeal for Peace, the Peace and Justice Studies Association and many, many others easily found by an internet search. World BEYOND War lists on its website hundreds of organizations and thousands of individuals from all over the world who have signed our pledge to work to end all war.

Both governmental and non-governmental organizations have established peacekeeping forces, such as the UN's Blue Helmets and several citizen-based, nonviolent models, such as Nonviolent Peaceforce and Peace Brigades International. Likewise, faith-based institutions have developed peace and justice commissions. At the same time, there has been a rapid growth of peace research and the expansion of the field of peace education at all levels. Other factors that have helped to advance the peace system include the spread of peace-oriented religions, the development of the world-wide web, the impossibility of global empires (too costly), the end of de-facto sovereignty, the growing acceptance of conscientious objection to war, new techniques of conflict resolution, peace journalism, the growth of the global conference movement (gatherings focusing on peace, justice, the environment, and development)[61], the environmental movement (including the efforts to end reliance on oil and oil-related wars), and the development of a sense of planetary loyalty.[62] [63] These are only a few of the significant trends that indicate a self-organizing, Alternative Global Security System is well on the way to development.

---

61. In the past twenty-five years, there have been seminal gatherings at the global level aimed at creating a peaceful and just world. This emergence of the global conference movement, initiated by the Earth Summit in Rio de Janeiro in Brazil in 1992, laid the foundations for the modern global conference movement. Focused on environment and development, it produced a dramatic shift toward the elimination of toxins in production, the development of alternative energy and public transportation, reforestation, and a new realization of the scarcity of water. Examples are: Earth Summit Rio 1992 on the environment and sustainable development; Rio+20 brought together thousands of participants from governments, the private sector, NGOs and other groups, to shape how humans can reduce poverty, advance social equity and ensure environmental protection on an ever more crowded planet; Triennial World Water Forum as the largest international event in the field of water to raise awareness on water issues and solutions (initiated 1997); The Hague Appeal for Peace Conference of 1999 as the largest international peace conference by civil society groups.

62. These trends are presented in-depth in the study guide "The Evolution of a Global Peace System" and the short documentary provided by the War Prevention Initiative at http://warpreventioninitiative.org/?page_id=2674

63. A 2016 survey found that almost half of the respondents across 14 tracking countries considered themselves more as global citizens than citizens of their country. See *Global Citizenship: A Growing Sentiment Among Citizens Of Emerging Economies: Global Poll* at http://globescan.com/news-and-analysis/press-releases/press-releases-2016/103-press-releases-2016/383-global-citizenship-a-growing-sentiment-among-citizens-of-

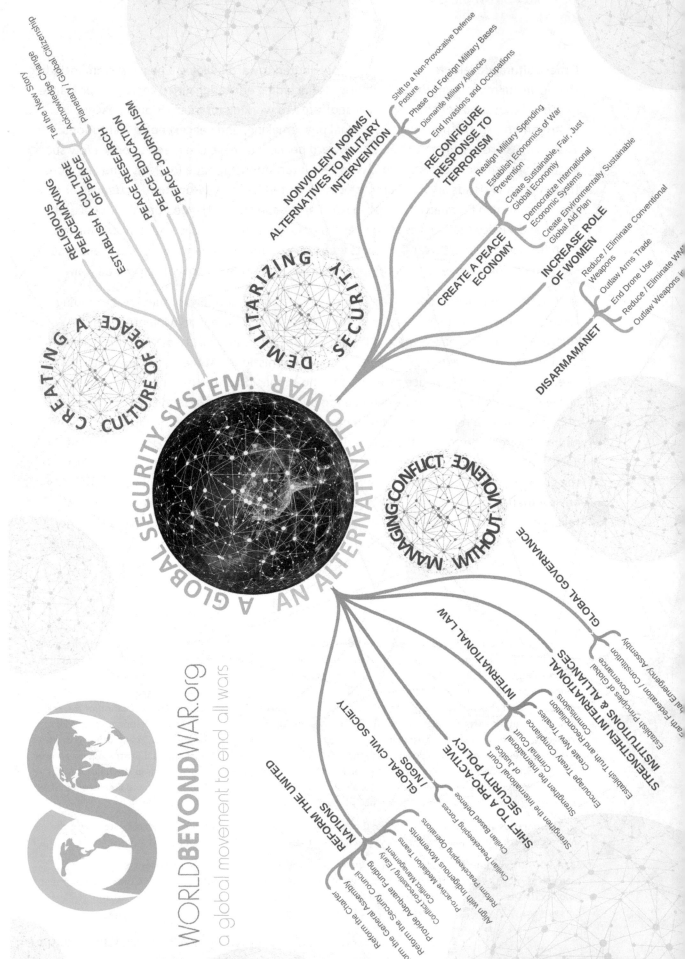

A GLOBAL SECURITY SYSTEM: AN ALTERNATIVE TO WAR

CREATING A CULTURE OF PEACE

- RELIGIOUS PEACEMAKING
  - Tell the New Story
  - Acknowledge / Global Citizenship
  - Planetary / Global Citizenship
- ESTABLISH A CULTURE OF PEACE
- PEACE RESEARCH
- PEACE EDUCATION
- PEACE JOURNALISM

DEMILITARIZING SECURITY

- NONVIOLENT NORMS / ALTERNATIVES TO MILITARY INTERVENTION
  - Shift to a Non-Provocative Defense Posture
  - Phase Out Foreign Military Bases
  - Dismantle Military Alliances
  - End Invasions and Occupations
- RECONFIGURE RESPONSE TO TERRORISM
- CREATE A PEACE ECONOMY
  - Realign Military Spending
  - Establish Economics of War Prevention
  - Create Sustainable, Fair, Just Global Economy
  - Democratize International Economic Systems
  - Create Environmentally Sustainable Global Aid Plan
- INCREASE ROLE OF WOMEN
- DISARMAMANET
  - Reduce / Eliminate Conventional Weapons
  - Outlaw Arms Trade
  - End Drone Use
  - Reduce / Eliminate WM
  - Outlaw Weapons in

MANAGING CONFLICT WITHOUT VIOLENCE

- GLOBAL GOVERNANCE
  - Earth Federation / Constitution
  - Establish Principles of Global Governance
  - bal Emergency Assembly
- STRENGTHEN INTERNATIONAL INSTITUTIONS & ALLIANCES
- INTERNATIONAL LAW
  - Create New Treaties
  - Encourage Treaty Compliance
  - Strengthen the International Criminal Court
  - Establish the International Court of Justice
  - Encourage Truth and Reconciliation Commissions
- SHIFT TO A PRO-ACTIVE SECURITY POLICY
  - Civilian Based Defense
  - Strengthen Peacekeeping Forces
- GLOBAL CIVIL SOCIETY / NGOS
  - Pro-active Indigenous Movements
  - Align with Indigenous Movements
- REFORM THE UNITED NATIONS
  - Reform the Charter
  - Reform the General Assembly
  - Provide Adequate Funding
  - Align with Security Council
  - Early Conflict Forecasting / Conflict Management
  - Civilian Peacekeeping Operations
  - Pro-active Mediation Teams

WORLDBEYONDWAR.org
a global movement to end all wars

WORLDBEYONDWAR.org
a global movement to end all wars

OUTLINE OF AN ALTERNATIVE GLOBAL SECURITY SYSTEM

No single strategy will end war. They must be layered and woven together to be effective. Entire books have been written about them, a few of which are listed in the Resources section in the Appendices. As will be apparent, choosing a World BEYOND War will require us to dismantle the existing War System and create the institutions of an Alternative Global Security System and/or to further develop them where they already exist in embryo. Note that World BEYOND War is not proposing a sovereign world government, but rather a web of governing structures voluntarily entered into, and a shift in cultural norms away from violence and domination.

HOW SYSTEMS WORK

A system is any set of "interconnected and mutually reinforcing structures or patterns that together govern the functioning and direction of a given entity"[64] toward a particular purpose. In other words, systems are webs of relationships in which each part influences the other parts through feedback. Point A not only influences point B, but B feeds back to A, and so on until points on the web are wholly interdependent. For example, in the War System, the military institution will influence education to set up Junior Reserve Officers' Training Corps (JROTC) programs in the high schools; the high school history courses will present war as patriotic, inescapable and normative; while churches pray for the troops and parishioners work in the arms industry; which Congress has funded in order to create jobs to increase their likelihood of re-election. Retired military officers will head the arms manufacturing companies and get contracts from their former institution, the Pentagon and/or make up many of the so-called media experts on war and peace issues. The latter scenario is what is infamously called the "military revolving door". A system is made up of interlocked beliefs, values, technologies, and above all, institutions that reinforce each other. While systems tend to be stable for long periods of time, if enough negative pressure develops, the system can reach a tipping point and can change rapidly.

We live in a war-peace continuum, shifting back and forth between stable war, unstable war, unstable peace, and stable peace[65]. Stable war is what we saw in Europe for centuries and now see in the Middle East since 1947. Stable peace is what we have seen in Scandinavia for hundreds of years (apart from Scandinavian participation in U.S./NATO wars). The U.S. hostility with Canada which saw five wars in the 17th and 18th centuries ended suddenly in 1815. Stable war changed rapidly to stable peace. These phase changes are real world changes but limited to specific regions. What World BEYOND War seeks is to apply phase change to the entire world, to move it from stable war to stable peace - within and between nations.

emerging-economies-global-poll.html

64. Hollins, H., Powers, A., & Sommer, M. (1989). *The conquest of war: Alternative strategies for global security.* Boulder, CO: Westview Press.

65. Boulding, K. (1978). *Stable peace.* Austin, TX: University of Texas Press.

"A global peace system is a condition of humankind's social system that reliably maintains peace. A variety of combinations of institutions, policies, habits, values, capabilities, and circumstances could produce this result... Such a system must evolve out of existing conditions."
- Robert A. Irwin (Professor of Sociology)

COMPONENTS OF THE ALTERNATIVE GLOBAL SECURITY SYSTEM

As previously mentioned, the Alternative Global Security System outlined here is pursued through three broad strategies: 1) demilitarizing security, 2) managing conflicts without violence, and 3) creating a culture of peace. These strategies are also utilized as the organizing components of our system.

Demilitarizing Security
This component identifies the strategies and approaches necessary for demilitarizing the current system.

Managing Conflict Without Violence
Here we explore possible reforms to existing institutions and approaches to maintaining security – and, where current options are deemed ineffective or insufficient, we propose alternative possibilities. These are the tools essential to pursuing a nonviolent approach to security.

Creating a Culture of Peace
Our system also depends upon identifying and establishing the social and cultural norms, values and principles of peace to guide our actions and vision of a more preferred world order. These principles also function as a litmus test to assess the validity of current and alternative approaches and proposals.

The development of these components are not necessarily to be pursued sequentially – or separately - as advancements in one area will almost certainly have reciprocating influences in other areas. Strategies will need adjusting as we observe these influences and impacts. It should be noted that many of the approaches could easily be situated within more than one category – their current placement reflects what we think to be the most logical and practical interrelationships.

WORLD**BEYOND**WAR.org
a global movement to end all wars

ALTERNATIVE GLOBAL SECURITY SYSTEM OUTLINE & OVERVIEW

Component	Demilitarizing Security	Managing Conflict Without Violence	Creating a Culture of Peace
Primary Function(s)	1.Demilitarize security. 2.Establish alternative security frameworks and alternative thinking that should shape the new system	1.Establish and reform institutions for managing international and civil conflicts	1.Establish normative frameworks, values and principles to guide the vision and assess alternative approaches to security 2.Establish operating principles for a culture of peace

Sub-Components, Approaches & Action Steps	•Identify / Establish Nonviolent Norms & Alternatives to Military Intervention
	
	  -Shift to a Non-Provocative Defense Posture
	
	  -Phase Out Foreign Military Bases
	
	  -Dismantle Military Alliances
	
	  -End Invasions & Occupations
	
	•Disarmament
	
	  -Conventional Weapons (reduction / elimination)
	
	  -Outlaw Arms Trade
	
	  -End Drone Use
	
	  -Phase out WMDs (nuclear, chemical, biological)
	
	  -Outlaw Weapons in Space
	
	•Create a Peace Economy
	
	  -Realign Military Spending (economic conversion)
	
	  -Establish an Economics of War Prevention
	
	  -Create a Stable, Fair and Sustainable Global Economy
	
	  -Democratize International Economic Institutions
	
	  -Create an Environmentally Sustainable Global Aid Plan
	
	•Reconfigure the Response to Terrorism
	
	•Increase the Role of Women in Peace and Security
		•Shift to a Pro-active Security Posture
		
		•Strengthen International Institutions and Regional Alliances
		
		•Reform the UN
		
		  -Reform the Charter
		
		  -Reform the General Assembly
		
		  -Reform the Security Council
		
		  -Provide Adequate Funding
		
		  -Increase Capacities for Conflict Forecasting & Early Management*
		
		  -Establish Pro-active Mediation Teams*
		
		  -Align with Indigenous Movements
		
		  -Reform Peacekeeping Operations*
		
		•International Law
		
		  -Strengthen the International Court of Justice
		
		  -Strengthen the International Criminal Court
		
		  -Encourage Compliance with Existing Treaties
		
		  -Create New Treaties*
		
		  -Establish Truth and Reconciliation Commissions
		
		•Support Nonviolent Intervention: Utilize Civilian Peacekeeping Forces*
		
		•Create a Nonviolent, Civilian-Based Defense Force*
		
		•Explore Alternative Approaches to Humane Global Governance
		
		  -Establish Principles of Humane Global Governance / Explore Alternative Models
		
		  -The Earth Federation & The Earth Constitution
		
		  -Global Emergency* Assembly*
		
		  •Identify / Increase the Role of Global Civil Society and International NGOs
			•Establish a Culture of Peace
			
			  -Tell The New Story
			
			  -Acknowledge Change
			
			•Nurture Planetary / Global Citizenship
			
			•Spread and Fund Peace Education and Peace Research
			
			•Cultivate Peace Journalism
			
			•Utilize Religion as a Tool for Building Peace

DEMILITARIZING SECURITY

EXECUTIVE SUMMARY

Our approach to demilitarizing security requires a rethinking of what makes us secure and alleviating our dependence on militarized approaches. We advocate for several essential strategies to move away from dependence on military intervention as a means to security. Many of these strategies are transitionary: shifting to a non-provocative defense posture, phasing our foreign military bases, dismantling military alliances, and ending invasions and occupations. Disarmament efforts are the backbone of this system component – thus we outline several rationales and strategies to support General and Complete Disarmament (GCD). Conventional, chemical and biological weapons, weapons of mass destruction, weapons in space, drones, and the arms trade are addressed here. As the present system is so deeply entrenched in the military-industrial-corporate-academic complex, we also address the challenge of transitioning to a peace economy. Here we identify strategies for economic conversion; creating a stable, just and environmentally sustainable economy; and democratizing international monetary institutions. Our system also supports the adoption of more effective nonviolent, demilitarized responses to terrorism. Finally, we conclude this section by highlighting the important strategy of increasing the role of women in peace and security decision making, planning and peacebuilding efforts.

STRATEGIC POLICY AND ACTION RECOMMENDATIONS

Transitionary Recommendations:

- Advocate all countries to shift to a non-provocative that requires the immediate phasing out of foreign military bases; dismantling military alliances; and ending all invasions and occupations.

- Encourage full compliance, from all countries, to existing disarmament treaties.

- Encourage individual, group, and institutional participation in divestment campaigns.

Transformative Recommendations:

- Make transition steps toward General and Complete Disarmament a fundamental requirement of all future disarmament treaties and agreements.

- Develop comprehensive strategies for economic conversion to aid the shift from a military economy to a pro-peace, sustainable economy.

- Assure full consideration of ecological and environmental security concerns in all security decision making (require short and long-term environmental assessments)

- Democratize international monetary institutions.

- Require a nonviolence first response, rooted in the rule of law, to all acts of terrorism (whether it be state sponsored terrorism or terrorism from below)

- Further increase the role and participation of women in peace and security decision-making and peacebuilding processes in compliance with UN Security Council Resolutions 1325 and 1820.

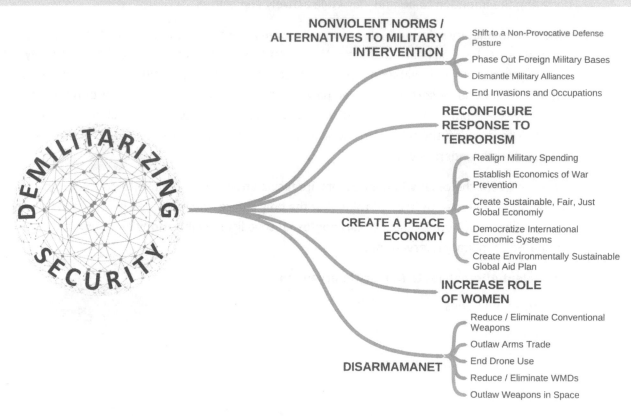

"Conflicts typical of the contemporary world cannot be resolved at gunpoint.
They require not a recalibration of military tools and strategies but a
far-reaching commitment to demilitarization."
- Tom Hastings (Author and Professor of Conflict Resolution)

"Military force is necessary to keep us secure." How often have we heard this argument from well-intended, good people? It is time to move beyond this argument and challenge the notion that military interventions should be used for the sake of peace and security. At a certain time, in a certain place, a certain group of people can be saved through a military intervention. How can we argue against that? We cannot. However, a military intervention will always make the overall situation worse and the prospects for constructive transformation of the conflict will shrink. Moreover, while lives might be saved somewhere, additional lives will be taken. And we have to face the reality. A military intervention will always take innocent lives.

A military intervention is the introduction of outside military forces into an existing conflict. This takes place through means including the introduction of weapons and arms, air strikes and combat troops to intervene in an armed conflict. It is the use of deadly force on a massive scale. Humanitarian intervention by any name is war, and wars are by nature destructive. There is violence, death and suffering. In other words, when we are talking about a humanitarian military intervention, we are talking about a complete oxymoron: declaring the intention to defend life, while actively taking lives.

"There is no military solution," "this cannot be solved militarily," "the solution has to be political" – We have all heard that many times. Yet those exact same phrases are commonly used to justify wars and military interventions. It is time to follow a new path. A path that is not informed by some sort of perceived naïve pacifism, but by rigorous analysis of nonviolent alternatives without a so-called military option as part of the picture. The military option needs to be taken off the table, otherwise all the other approaches are facing a counterforce and are directly undermined.

But what about the cases when innocents are facing atrocities? We have to do something, right? Absolutely. Let us just not think that the only choices we have are either a military intervention or inaction. Consider this non-exhaustive list of viable, nonviolent alternatives compared to military intervention:[66]

Nonviolent Alternatives to Military Intervention

- Arms embargoes

- End all military aid

- Civil society support, nonviolent actors

- Sanctions

- Work through supranational bodies (e.g. UN, ICC)

- Ceasefires

- Aid to refugees (relocate/improve proximal camps/repatriate)

- Pledge no use of violence

- Withdrawal of military

- Nonviolent conflict workers

- (Transitional) justice initiatives

- Meaningful diplomacy

- Conflict resolution framework

- Inclusive good governance

- Confront violence supporting beliefs

---

66. These points are taken from the Peace and Security Funders Group 2015 annual meeting, where Patrick Hiller debated on a panel: "Military intervention should never be used for the sake of peace and security."

- Increasing women's participation in social and political life

- Accurate information on facts

- Separate perpetrators from support base – addressing the grey area

- Ban war profiteering

- Peacebuilding engagement; reframe the either/or us/them choices

- Effective policing

- Nonviolent civil resistance

- Information gathering and reporting

- Public advocacy

- Conciliation, arbitration and judicial settlement

- Human rights mechanisms

- Humanitarian assistance and protection

- Economic, political and strategic inducements

- Monitoring, observation and verification

- Divestment

- International law

Many of the concepts are familiar. If they are not applied, it is not because they are unavailable, but because of artificially imposed constraints, lack of interest, or self-interest. While no magical solutions, we know they work. We have to look at them in terms of effectiveness versus the military intervention. And it is beyond doubt that they are more effective as short, medium, and long-term responses.

SHIFT TO A NON-PROVOCATIVE DEFENSE POSTURE

A first step toward demilitarizing security could be non-provocative defense, which is to reconceive and reconfigure training, logistics, doctrine, and weaponry so that a nation's military is seen by its neighbors to be unsuitable for offense but clearly able to mount a credible defense of its borders. It is a form of defense that rules out armed attacks against other states.

"Can the weapon system be effectively used abroad, or can it be only used at home? If it can be used abroad, then it is offensive, particularly if that 'abroad' includes countries with which one is in conflict. It if can only be used at home then the system is defensive, being operational only when an attack has taken place."
- Johan Galtung, (Pioneering Peace Researcher) [67]

Non-provocative defense implies a truly defensive military posture. It includes radically reducing or eliminating long-range weapons such as Intercontinental Ballistic Missiles, long-range attack aircraft, carrier fleets and heavy ships, militarized drones, nuclear submarine fleets, overseas bases, and possibly tank armies. In a mature Alternative Global Security System, a militarized non-provocative defense posture would be gradually phased out as it became unnecessary.

Another defensive posture that will be necessary is a system of defense against futuristic attacks including cyber-attacks on the energy grid, power plants, communications, financial transactions and defense against dual-use technologies such as nanotechnology and robotics. Ramping up the cyber capabilities of Interpol would be a first line of defense in this case and another element of an Alternative Global Security System.[68]

Also, non-provocative defense would not rule out a nation having long-range aircraft and ships configured exclusively for humanitarian relief. Shifting to non-provocative defense weakens the War System while making possible the creation of a humanitarian disaster relief force that strengthens the peace system.

Phase Out Foreign Military Bases

In 2009 the U.S. lease on an air base in Ecuador was set to expire and the president of Ecuador made a proposal to the U.S.: "We'll renew the base on one condition: that they let us put a base in Miami." The U.S. refused the offer.

The British people would find it unthinkable if their government allowed Saudi Arabia to establish a large military base in the British Isles. Similarly, the United States would not tolerate an Iranian air base in Wyoming. These foreign establishments would be seen as a threat to their security, their safety and their sovereignty. Foreign military bases are valuable

---

67. This statement by John Galtung is put into context by himself, when he suggests that defensive weapons are still highly violent, but that there is reason to be optimistic that such a path of transarmament from conventional military defense will develop into nonviolent non-military defense. See complete paper at: https://www.transcend.org/galtung/papers/Transarmament-From%20Offensive%20to%20Defensive%20Defense.pdf

68. Interpol is the International Criminal Police Organization, set up in 1923, as an NGO facilitating international police cooperation.

for controlling populations and resources. They are locations from which the occupying power can strike inside the "host" country or against nations on its borders, or possibly deter attacks. They are also frightfully expensive for the occupying country. The United States is the prime example, having hundreds of bases in 135 countries around the world. Foreign bases create resentment against what is seen locally as imperial domination. Eliminating foreign military bases is a pillar of an Alternative Global Security System and goes hand-in hand with non-provocative defense.

Withdrawing to an authentic defense of a nation's borders is a key part of demilitarizing security, thus weakening the ability of the War System to create global insecurity. As an alternative, some of the bases could be converted to civilian use in a "Global Aid Plan" as country assistance centers (see below). Others could be converted to solar panel arrays and other systems of sustainable energy.

Current Action Campaigns: Phasing out Foreign Bases

World BEYOND War is playing a leadership role in the creation of a new coalition that will work in the United States and in partnership with people around the world on closing U.S. military bases outside the United States.

The coalition is here: www.noforeignbases.org
Information from World BEYOND War is here: https://worldbeyondwar.org/bases
Maps showing where bases can be found are here: https://worldbeyondwar.org/militarism-mapped/

Dismantle Military Alliances

Military alliances such as the North Atlantic Treaty Organization (NATO) are leftovers from the Cold War. With the collapse of the Soviet client states in Eastern Europe, the Warsaw Pact alliance disappeared, but NATO expanded up to the borders of the former Soviet Union in violation of a promise to former premier Gorbachev, and has resulted in extreme tension between Russia and the West— the beginnings of a new Cold War–signaled perhaps by a U.S.-supported coup in Ukraine; the Russian annexation of, or reunification with, the Crimea - depending on which narrative prevails - and the civil war in Ukraine. This new cold war could too easily become a nuclear war which could kill hundreds of millions of people. NATO is a positive reinforcement of the War System, reducing rather than creating security. NATO has also taken on military exercises well beyond the borders of Europe. It has become a force for militarized efforts in Eastern Europe, North Africa and the Middle East.

End Invasions and Occupations

The occupation of one people by another is a major threat to security and peace, resulting in direct, structural and cultural violence that often prompts the occupied to mount various levels of attacks from "terrorist" assaults to guerrilla warfare. Prominent examples are: Israel's occupation of the West Bank and assaults on Gaza, and China's occupation of Tibet. Even though the strong U.S. military presence in Germany, and even more so in Japan, some 70 years after World War II, has not resulted in a violent response, it does create resentment, as do U.S. troops in many of the 175 nations where they are now based.

Even when the invading and occupying power has overwhelming military capability, these adventures usually do not work out due to several factors. First, they are enormously expensive. Second, they are often pitted against those who have a greater stake in the conflict because they are fighting to protect their homeland. Third, even "victories," as in Iraq, are elusive and leave the countries devastated and politically fractured. Fourth, once in, it's hard to get out, as the U.S. invasion of Afghanistan exemplifies; an invasion which officially "ended" in December, 2014 after thirteen years, although almost 10,000 U.S. troops remain in country. Finally, and foremost, invasions and armed occupations against resistance kill more civilians than resistance fighters and create millions of refugees.

Invasions are outlawed by the UN Charter, unless they are in retaliation for a prior invasion, which we argue is an inadequate and immoral provision. The presence of troops of one country inside another with or without an invitation destabilizes global security and makes conflicts more likely to be militarized and would be prohibited in an Alternative Global Security System.

DISARMAMENT

Disarmament is an obvious step leading toward a world beyond war. The problem of war is in great measure a problem of wealthy nations flooding poor nations with weapons, most of them for a profit, others for free. Regions of the world that we think of as war-prone,

Meet Study and Action Partners Ann Wright and Kozue Akibayashi: Disarmament and Demilitarization Activists

Ann Wright was in the U.S. Army/Army Reserves for 29 years and retired as a Colonel. She also served as a U.S. diplomat for 16 years in US Embassies around the world. She resigned from the U.S. government in March 2003 in opposition to Bush's war on Iraq. Since then she has worked for peace around the world with Veterans For Peace, CODEPINK: Women for Peace, and Afghan Peace Volunteers among many groups. She is the co-author of Dissent: Voices of Conscience. Ann is featured in a video on Study War No More introducing a discussion on what a demilitarized, defensive form of global security might look like and how might we make the transition. Join the discussion and check out Ann's video here: http://bit.ly/StudyWarNoMore7

Kozue Akibayashi is a feminist peace researcher activist and the International President of the Women's International League for Peace and Freedom. Kozue's activism and research has focused on militarism and demilitarization of security from a gender perspective. She has been active in several transnational feminist peace movements including the International Women's Network against Militarism, which calls for demilitarization and decolonization of security, and Women Cross DMZ for peace on the Korean Peninsula. Kozue is featured in a video on Study War No More introducing a discussion how we might pursue the practical and urgent necessity of disarmament, while also engaging in the transformative work of demilitarizing global security. Join the discussion and check out Kozue's video here: http://bit.ly/StudyWarNoMore8

including Africa and most of Western Asia, do not manufacture most of their own weapons. They import them from distant, wealthy nations. International small arms sales, in particular, have skyrocketed in recent years, tripling since 2001.[69]

The United States is the world's leading weapons seller. Most of the rest of international weapons sales come from the four other permanent members of the United Nations Security Council plus Germany. If these six countries stopped dealing weapons, global disarmament would be a very long way toward success.

The violence of poor countries is often used to justify war (and arms sales) in wealthy countries. Many wars have U.S.-made weapons on both sides. Some have U.S. trained and armed proxies on both sides, as has been the case lately in Syria where troops armed by the Department of Defense have fought troops armed by the CIA. The typical response is not disarmament, but more armament, more weapons gifts and sales to proxies, and more arms purchases in the wealthy nations.

The United States is not just the biggest arms seller, but also the biggest arms buyer. Were the United States to scale back its arsenal, removing various weapons systems that lack a defensive purpose, for example, a reverse arms race might be kick-started.

Efforts to end war are crippled by the ongoing existence and growth of the arms trade, but scaling back and ending the arms trade is a possible path toward ending war. Strategically, this approach has some possible advantages. For example, opposing U.S. weapons sales to Saudi Arabia or gifts to Egypt or Israel does not require a confrontation with U.S. patriotism in the way that opposing U.S. wars does. Instead we can confront the arms trade as the global health threat that it is.

Disarmament will require reductions in so-called conventional weapons as well as nuclear and other weapons types. We will need to end profiteering in arms trading. We will need to restrain the aggressive pursuit of global dominance that leads other nations to acquire nuclear weapons as deterrents. But we will also need to take on disarmament step-by-step, eliminating particular systems, such as armed drones, nuclear, chemical, and biological weapons, and weapons in outer space.

Conventional Weapons

The world is awash in armaments, everything from automatic weapons to battle tanks and heavy artillery. The flood of arms contributes both to the escalation of violence in wars and to the dangers of crime and terrorism. It aids governments that have committed gross human rights abuses, creates international instability, and perpetuates the belief that peace can be achieved by guns.

---

69. For relevant data, see World BEYOND War's "Militarism Mapped" online tool: https://worldbeyondwar. org/militarism-mapped/

A Global Security System: An Alternative to War 2018-19 Edition

The United Nations Office for Disarmament Affairs (UNODA) is guided by the vision of promoting global norms of disarmament and oversees efforts to deal with weapons of mass destruction, conventional arms, and the arms trade.[70] The office promotes nuclear disarmament and non-proliferation; strengthening of the disarmament regimes in respect to other weapons of mass destruction, including chemical and biological weapons; and disarmament efforts in the area of conventional weapons, especially landmines and small arms, which are the weapons of choice in contemporary conflicts.

Outlaw the Arms Trade

Arms manufacturers have lucrative government contracts and are even subsidized by them and also sell on the open market. The U.S. and others have sold billions in arms into the volatile and violent Middle East. Sometimes the arms are sold to both sides in a conflict, as in the case of Iraq and Iran and the war between them that killed between 600,000 and 1,250,000 based on scholarly estimates.[71] Sometimes weapons end up being used against the seller or its allies, as in the case of weapons the U.S. provided to the Mujahedeen, which ended up in the hands of al Qaeda, and the arms the U.S. sold or gave to Iraq, which ended up in the hands of ISIS during its 2014 invasion of Iraq.

The international trade in death-dealing weapons is huge, over $70 billion per year. The main exporters of arms to the world are the powers that fought in World War II; in order: U.S., Russia, Germany, France, and the United Kingdom.

The UN adopted the Arms Trade Treaty (ATT) on April 2, 2013. It does not abolish the international arms trade. The treaty is an "instrument establishing common international standards for the import, export and transfer of conventional arms." It entered into force in December 2014. In the main, it says the exporters will monitor themselves to avoid selling arms to "terrorists or rogue states." The U.S., which has not ratified the treaty, nonetheless made certain that it had a veto over the text by demanding that consensus govern the deliberations. The U.S. demanded that the treaty leave huge loopholes so that the treaty will not "unduly interfere with our ability to import, export, or transfer arms in support of our national security and foreign policy interests" [and] "the international arms trade is a legitimate commercial activity" [and] "otherwise lawful commercial trade in arms must not be unduly hindered." Further, "There is no requirement for reporting on or marking and tracing of ammunition or explosives [and] there will be no mandate for an international body to enforce an ATT."[72]

---

70. See UNODO website at http://www.un.org/disarmament/

71. War casualty estimates are almost always contested. See: "Iran and Iraq remember war that cost more than a million lives". https://www.theguardian.com/world/2010/sep/23/iran-iraq-war-anniversary. See also: Hiro, Dilip (1991). The longest war: The Iran–Iraq military conflict. New York: Routledge.

72. See "Key U.S. Redlines in the Negotiations: https://2009-2017.state.gov/t/isn/armstradetreaty/index.htm

An Alternative Security System requires a major level of disarmament in order for all nations to feel safe from aggression. The UN defines general and complete disarmament as "the elimination of all WMD," coupled with the "balanced reduction of armed forces and conventional armaments, based on the principle of undiminished security of the parties with a view to promoting or enhancing stability at a lower military level, taking into account the need of all States to protect their security."[73] This definition of disarmament seems to have holes large enough to drive a tank through. A much more aggressive treaty with dated reduction levels is required, as well as an enforcement mechanism.

The Treaty appears to do no more than require States Parties to create an agency to oversee arms exports and imports and to determine if they think the arms will be misused for such activities as genocide or piracy and to report annually on their trade. It does not appear to do the job since it leaves the control of the trade up to those who want to export and import. A far more vigorous and enforceable ban on the export of arms is necessary. The arms trade needs to be added to the International Criminal Court's list of "crimes against humanity" and enforced in the case of individual arms manufacturers and traders and by the Security Council in its mandate to confront violations of "international peace and security" in the case of sovereign states as the selling agents.[74]

End the Use of Militarized Drones

Photo: Armed Predatordrone firing Hellfire missile

Drones are pilotless aircraft (as well as submarines and other robots) maneuvered remotely from a distance of thousands of miles. Thus far, the main deployer of military drones

---

73. UN General Assembly, Final Document of the First Special Session on Disarmament (1978), para. 22. http://www.un.org/en/ga/search/view_doc.asp?symbol=a/res/S-10/2

74. Article 7 of the Rome Statute of the International Criminal Court identifies the crimes against humanity.

has been the United States. "Predator" and "Reaper" drones carry rocket-propelled high explosive warheads which can be targeted on people. They are maneuvered by "pilots" sitting at computer terminals in Nevada and elsewhere. These drones are regularly used for so-called targeted killings against people in Pakistan, Yemen, Afghanistan, Somalia, Iraq, and Syria. The justification for these attacks, which have killed hundreds of civilians, is the highly questionable doctrine of "anticipatory defense." The U.S. President has determined that he can, with the aid of a special panel, order the death of anyone deemed to be a terrorist threat to the U.S., even U.S. citizens for whom the Constitution requires due process of law, conveniently ignored in this case.[75] In fact, the U.S. Constitution requires respect of the rights of all, not just U.S. citizens as we are commonly taught. And among the targeted are people never identified, but deemed "suspicious" by their behavior, a parallel to racial profiling by domestic police.

Tracking U.S. Drone Warfare

The Bureau of Investigative Journalism has been tracking U.S. drone strikes around the world. There is little surprise that their numbers are significantly greater than official U.S. accounts.

Current Statistics (July 2018)
4,926 - MINIMUM CONFIRMED STRIKES
7,715-11,067 - TOTAL KILLED
751-1,555 - CIVILIANS KILLED
252-345 - CHILDREN KILLED

The figures above are running totals of US actions and resulting deaths since the Bureau began recording data. For the most current data visit:
https://www.thebureauinvestigates.com/projects/drone-war

The problems with drone attacks are legal, moral, and practical. To begin with, they are a clear violation of every nation's laws against murder. Additionally, they violate U.S. law, issued as executive orders under President Gerald Ford and President Ronald Reagan, outlawing assassinations by the U.S. government. Used against U.S. citizens, or anyone else, these killings violate the rights of due process under the U.S. Constitution. And while current international law under Article 51 of the UN Charter legalizes self-defense in the case of an armed attack, drones nevertheless appear to violate international law as well as the Geneva Conventions. While drones might be considered legally used in a combat zone in a declared war, the U.S. has not declared war in all of the countries where it kills with drones, nor are any of its current wars legal under the U.N. Charter or the Kellogg-Briand Pact, nor is it clear what makes certain wars "declared" as the U.S. Congress has not declared war since 1941.

---

75. See: www.theguardian.com/world/2013/may/24/obama-drone-vetting-kill-courts

First, the doctrine of anticipatory defense, which states that a nation can legitimately use force when it anticipates that it might be attacked, is questioned by many international law experts. The problem with such an interpretation of international law is its ambiguity—how does a nation know for certain that what another state or non-state actor says and does would truly lead to an armed attack? In fact, any would-be aggressor could actually hide behind this doctrine to justify its aggression. At the least, it could be (and is presently) used indiscriminately without oversight by Congress or the United Nations.

Second, drone attacks are clearly immoral even under the conditions of "just war doctrine" which stipulates that non-combatants are not to be attacked in warfare. Many of the drone attacks are not targeted on known individuals whom the government designates as terrorists[76], but simply against gatherings where such people are suspected to be present. Many civilians have been killed in these attacks and there is evidence that on some occasions, when rescuers have gathered at the site after the first attack, a second strike has been ordered to kill the rescuers. Many of the dead have been children.[77]

Third, drone attacks are counter-productive. While purporting to kill enemies of the U.S. (a sometimes dubious claim), they create intense resentment for the U.S. and are easily used in recruiting new terrorists.

> *"For every innocent person you kill, you create ten new enemies."*
> *- General Stanley McChrystal (former Commander, U.S. and NATO*
> *Forces in Afghanistan)*

Further, by arguing that its drone attacks are legal even when war has not been declared, the U.S provides justification for other nations or groups to claim legality when they may well want to use drones to attack the U.S. Drone attacks make a nation that uses them less, rather than more, secure.

---

76. Many who are targeted are not officially identified as having engaged in terrorist activities but deemed "suspicious" by their behavior. These U.S. "signature strikes" are based on two "suspicious behavior" criteria: carrying a weapon, and being a military age male. Nothing about meeting such criteria qualifies as "suspicious." The convenient labelling of someone as "terrorist" (or substitute "combatant," "militant," or "extremist") is used all the time as justification for killing. Further, by categorizing "suspicious" males as "terrorists" their death is no longer considered a "civilian" death which whitewashes the casualty statistics.

77. The comprehensive report "*Living Under Drones. Death, Injury and Trauma to Civilians from U.S. Drone Practices in Pakistan*" (2012) by the Stanford International Human Rights and Conflict Resolution Clinic and the Global Justice Clinic at NYU School of Law demonstrates that the U.S. narratives of "targeted killings" is false. The report shows that civilians are injured and killed, drone strikes cause considerable harm to the daily lives of civilians, the evidence that strikes have made the U.S. safer is ambiguous at best, and that drone strike practices have undermined international law. The full report can be read here: http://www.livingunderdrones.org/wp-content/uploads/2013/10/Stanford-NYU-Living-Under-Drones.pdf

"When you drop a bomb from a drone… you are going to cause more
damage than you are going to cause good."
- U.S. Lt. General Michael Flynn (ret.)

More than seventy nations now possess drones, and more than 50 countries are developing them.[78] The rapid development of the technology and production capacity suggest that almost every nation will be able to have armed drones within a decade. Some War System advocates have said that the defense against drone attacks will be to build drones that attack drones, demonstrating the way in which War System thinking typically leads to arms races and greater instability, while widening the destruction when a particular war breaks out. Outlawing militarized drones by any and all nations and groups would be a major step forward in demilitarizing security.

"Drones are not named Predators and Reapers for nothing. They are killing
machines. With no judge or jury, they obliterate lives in an instant, the lives
of those deemed by someone, somewhere, to be terrorists, along with those
who are accidentally—or incidentally—caught in their crosshairs."
- Medea Benjamin (Activist, Author, Co-founder of CODEPINK)

Phase Out Weapons of Mass Destruction

Weapons of mass destruction are a powerful positive feedback to the war system, strengthening its spread and ensuring that wars that do occur have the potential for planet-altering destruction. Nuclear, chemical and biological weapons are characterized by their ability to kill and maim enormous numbers of people, wiping out whole cities and even whole regions with indescribable destruction.

Nuclear Weapons

Nuclear weapons are a threat to humanity and life on the planet. Recent years have been full of worry and hope. On the one hand, in 2017, we witnessed how 122 United Nations non-nuclear member states adopted a new legally binding Treaty on the Prohibition on Nuclear Weapons.[79] As of July 2018, the treaty has been signed by 59 countries, and ratified by 14,[80] 50 countries are required to ratify the treaty for it to enter into force. On the other hand,

---

78. See the report *Armed and Dangerous*. UAVs and U.S. Security by the Rand Corporation at: http://www.rand. org/content/dam/rand/pubs/research_reports/RR400/RR449/RAND_RR449.pdf

79. Treaty adopted on 7 July 2017. United Nations Conference to Negotiate a Legally Binding Instrument to Prohibit Nuclear Weapons, Leading Towards their Total Elimination. See: https://www.un.org/disarmament/ ptnw/index.html

80. www.icanw.org/status-of-the-treaty-on-the-prohibition-of-nuclear-weapons/

we are witnessing heightened tensions between nuclear-armed nations, most notably the escalatory moves and countermoves between the U.S. and North Korea, the U.S. backing out of the nuclear deal with Iran, and the deteriorating relationship between the U.S. and Russia. The U.S. and Russia have some 14,000 of the 15,000 nuclear bombs on the planet, with more than 2,000 in each country pointed at each other's major cities, ready to fire in minutes. We need advocacy and pressure on all levels against further short-term escalations, as well as long-term engagement on controlling weapons in space, ending NATO expansion to Russia's borders, removing U.S. missiles from Romania and Poland, and reinstituting the 1972 Anti-Ballistic Missile Treaty the U.S. had with the USSR and which George Bush walked out on in 2001. Only then, will we be able to create the negotiating conditions that would support the abolition of nuclear weapons once and for all.

The new ban treaty fills a significant gap in international law, prohibiting nations from developing, testing, producing, manufacturing, transferring, possessing, stockpiling, using or threatening to use nuclear weapons, or allowing nuclear weapons to be stationed on their territory. It also prohibits them from assisting, encouraging or inducing anyone to engage in any of these activities.[81] No nuclear weapons states, or nuclear "umbrella states" in the US nuclear alliance[82], joined the treaty.

The ban treaty is expected to stigmatize the bomb and put pressure not only on the nuclear

---

81. See "The Treaty" at http://www.icanw.org/the-treaty/

82. Including countries in NATO as well as Australia, South Korea and Japan

A Global Security System: An Alternative to War 2018-19 Edition

weapons states, but on the governments sheltered under the U.S. nuclear umbrella, which rely on nuclear weapons for "deterrence."[83] Additionally, the U.S. stations about 400 nuclear bombs in NATO states, Belgium, the Netherlands, Italy, Germany and Turkey, who will also be pressured to give up their "nuclear sharing arrangements" and sign the ban treaty.[84] [85] A "Don't Bank on the Bomb Campaign" is taking advantage of the new ban treaty to promote divestment campaigns around the world from investments in nuclear weapons manufacturers.[86]

The Treaty on the Prohibition on Nuclear Weapons was long overdue, given that there already were treaties banning biological and chemical weapons. The 1970 Non-Proliferation Treaty (NPT) provides that five recognized nuclear weapons states– the U.S., Russia, UK, France and China– should make good faith efforts for the elimination of nuclear weapons, while all other NPT signatories pledge not to acquire nuclear weapons. Only three countries refused to join the NPT— India, Pakistan, and Israel— and they acquired nuclear arsenals. North Korea, relying on the NPT bargain for "peaceful" nuclear technology, walked out of the treaty using its "peaceful" technology to develop fissile materials for nuclear power to manufacture nuclear bombs.[87] Indeed, every nuclear power plant is a potential bomb factory.

A war fought with even a so-called "limited" number of nuclear weapons would kill millions, induce nuclear winter and result in worldwide food shortages that would result in the starvation of millions. The whole nuclear strategy system rests upon a false foundation, because computer models suggest that only a very small percentage of warheads detonated could cause the worldwide shutdown of agriculture for up to a decade—in effect, a death sentence for the human species. And the trend at present is toward a greater and greater likelihood of some systemic failure of equipment or communication that would lead to nuclear weapons being used.

A larger release could extinguish all life on the planet. These weapons threaten the security of everyone everywhere.[88] While various nuclear arms control treaties between the U.S. and the former Soviet Union did reduce the insane number of nuclear weapons (56,000 at one point), there are still 15,000 in the world, only 1,000 of which are not in the U.S. or Russia.[89] What is worse, the treaties allowed for "modernization," a euphemism for creating a new

83. http://www.paxchristi.net/sites/default/files/nuclearweaponstimeforabolitionfinal.pdf

84. See: http://en.wikipedia.org/wiki/Nuclear_sharing; and https://www.armscontrol.org/act/2012_06/NATO_Sticks_With_Nuclear_Policy

85. A citizen initiative by PAX in the Netherlands calls for a ban of nuclear weapons in the Netherlands. Read the proposal at: http://www.paxforpeace.nl/media/files/pax-proposal-citizens-initiatiative-2016-eng.pdf.

86. https://www.dontbankonthebomb.com/

87. http://en.wikipedia.org/wiki/Treaty_on_the_Non-Proliferation_of_Nuclear_Weapons

88. See the report by Nobel Peace Laureate Organization International Physicians for the Prevention of Nuclear War "Nuclear Famine: two billion people at risk"

89. ibid

generation of weapons and delivery systems, which all of the nuclear states are doing. The nuclear monster has not gone away; it is not even lurking in the back of the cave—it's out in the open and costing billions of dollars that could be far better used elsewhere. Since the not so Comprehensive Test Ban Treaty was signed in 1998, the US has ramped up its high-tech laboratory tests of nuclear weapons, coupled with sub-critical tests, 1,000 feet below the desert floor at the Nevada test site on Western Shoshone land. The US has performed 28 such tests to date, blowing up plutonium with chemicals, without causing a chain-reaction, hence "sub-critical".[90] Indeed, the U.S., under President Obama, projected expenditures of one trillion dollars over the next thirty years for new bomb factories and delivery systems - voted on and passed by Congress during the Trump administration while upping the ante to include "smaller" more usable nuclear weapons. These" smaller" bombs have the fire power of the weapons that destroyed Hiroshima and Nagasaki, killing tens of thousands of people with one bomb.[91][92]

Conventional war system thinking argues that nuclear weapons deter war–the so-called doctrine of "Mutual Assured Destruction" ("MAD"). While it is true that they have not been used since 1945, it is not logical to conclude that MAD has been the reason. As Daniel Ellsberg has pointed out, every U.S. president since Truman has used nuclear weapons as a threat to other nations to get them to allow the U.S. to get its way. Furthermore, such a doctrine rests on a wobbly faith in the rationality of political leaders in a crisis situation, for all time to come. MAD does not ensure security against either accidental release of these monstrous weapons or a strike by a nation that mistakenly thought it was under attack or a pre-emptive first strike. In fact, certain kinds of nuclear warhead delivery systems have been designed and built for the latter purpose—the Cruise Missile (which sneaks under radar) and the Pershing Missile, a fast attack, forward-based missile. Serious discussions actually occurred during the Cold War about the desirability of a "Grand, Decapitating First Strike" in which the U.S. would initiate a nuclear attack on the Soviet Union in order to disable its ability to launch nuclear weapons by obliterating command and control, beginning with the Kremlin. Some analysts wrote about "winning" a nuclear war in which only a few tens of millions would be killed, nearly all civilians.[93] Nuclear weapons are patently immoral and insane.

Even if they are not used deliberately, there have been numerous incidents where nuclear weapons carried in airplanes have crashed to the ground, fortunately only spewing some plutonium on the ground, but not going off.[94] In 2007, six U.S. missiles carrying nuclear warheads were mistakenly flown from North Dakota to Louisiana and the missing nuclear

90. ibid

91. https://thinkprogress.org/trump-budget-low-yield-nuclear-weapons/

92. U.S. Nuclear Modernization Programs: https://www.armscontrol.org/factsheets/USNuclearModernization

93. http://www.nytimes.com/2014/09/22/us/us-ramping-up-major-renewal-in-nuclear-arms.html?_r=0

94. http://www.strategicstudiesinstitute.army.mil/pdffiles/pub585.pdf

A Global Security System: An Alternative to War 2018-19 Edition

bombs were not discovered for 36 hours.[95] There have been reports of drunkenness and poor performance by servicemen posted in underground silos responsible for launching U.S. nuclear missiles poised on hair-trigger alert and pointed at Russian cities.[96] The U.S. and Russia each have thousands of nuclear missiles primed and ready to be fired at each other. A Norwegian weather satellite went off-course over Russia and was almost taken for an incoming attack until the last minute when utter chaos was averted.[97]

Nuclear Weapons Free Zones hold some promise for denuclearization. These zones are defined by the United Nations as an agreement which a group of states has freely established by treaty or conventions that bans the use of nuclear weapons in a given area; has mechanisms for verification and control to enforce its obligations; and is recognized by the United Nations General Assembly. Zones were first developed over the Antarctic region, space, and Latin America and the Caribbean.[98] Today they are six land zones, which cover 56% of the Earth under such treaties, thus 60% of the 195 states on Earth. There are now efforts to develop a Nuclear Weapons Free Zone in the Korean Peninsula and the United Nations General Assembly has urged the establishment of a Nuclear Weapons Free Zone in the Middle East.[99] In the Middle East, such a treaty would cover nuclear, chemical, and biological weapons and be called a Weapons of Mass Destruction-Free Zone.[100]

> *"History does not make us, we make it—or end it."*
> *- Thomas Merton (Catholic Writer)*

Chemical and Biological Weapons

Biological weapons consist of deadly natural toxins such as Ebola, typhus, smallpox, and others that have been altered in the lab to be super virulent so there is no antidote. Their use could start an uncontrolled global epidemic. Therefore, it is critical to adhere to existing treaties that already make up part of an Alternative Global Security System. The Convention on the Prohibition of the Development, Production and Stockpiling of Bacteriological (Biological) and Toxin Weapons and on their Destruction was opened for signature in 1972 and went into force in 1975 under the aegis of the United Nations. It prohibits the 170

---

95. http://en.wikipedia.org/wiki/List_of_military_nuclear_accidents

96. http://en.wikipedia.org/wiki/2007_United_States_Air_Force_nuclear_weapons_incident

97. http://cdn.defenseone.com/defenseone/interstitial.html?v=2.1.1&rf=http%3A%2F%2Fwww.defenseone.com%2Fideas%2F2014%2F11%2Flast-thing-us-needs-are-mobile-nuclear-missiles%2F98828%2F

98. www.un.org/disarmament/wmd/nuclear/nwfz/ & www.armscontrol.org/factsheets/nwfz

99. At the Nuclear Proliferation Treaty Review Conferences of 1995 and 2010

100. For comprehensive information and data see the website of the Organization for the Prohibition of Chemical Weapons, which received the 2013 Nobel Peace Prize for its extensive efforts to eliminate chemical weapons.

signatories from possessing, developing, or stockpiling these weapons. However, it lacks a verification mechanism and needs to be strengthened by a rigorous challenge inspection protocol (i.e., any State can challenge another which has agreed in advance to an inspection).

The Convention on the Prohibition of the Development, Production, Stockpiling and Use of Chemical Weapons and on their Destruction prohibits the development, production, acquisition, stockpiling, retention, transfer or use of chemical weapons. States signatories have agreed to destroy stockpiles of chemical weapons they may hold and any facilities which produced them, as well as any chemical weapons they abandoned on the territory of other States in the past, and to create a challenge verification regime for certain toxic chemicals and their precursors in order to ensure that such chemicals are only used for purposes not prohibited. The convention entered into force on April 29, 1997. Whereas the world stockpiles of chemical weapons have been dramatically reduced, complete destruction is still a distant goal.[101] The treaty was successfully implemented in 2014, when Syria turned over its stockpiles of chemical weapons. The decision to pursue that result was made by U.S. President Barack Obama shortly after he reversed his decision to launch a major bombing campaign over Syria, the nonviolent disarmament measure serving as something of a public substitute for a war measure prevented largely by public pressure.

Outlaw Weapons in Outer Space

Several countries have developed plans and even hardware for warfare in outer space, including ground-to-space and space-to-space weapons to attack satellites, and space-to-ground weapons (including laser weapons) to attack Earth installations from space. In 2005 George W. Bush encouraged the development of an Air Force program called "rods from God": a hypothetical system of space-based tungsten rods that could hit a city with the explosive power of an intercontinental ballistic missile. In 2018 Donald Trump doubled down and proposed creating a new branch of the United States military dedicated to securing U.S. supremacy in space. In 1997, believing it had the lead in this type of weapons R&D, former Assistant Secretary of the United States Air Force for Space, Keith R. Hall, said, "with regard to space dominance, we have it, we like it and we're going to keep it."[102]

The dangers of placing weapons in outer space are obvious, especially in the case of nuclear weapons or advanced technology weapons. 130 nations now have space programs and there are 3,000 operational satellites in space. The dangers include undermining existing weapons conventions and starting a new arms race. If such a space-based war were to occur the consequences would be terrifying for earth's inhabitants, as well as risking the dangers of the Kessler Syndrome, a scenario in which the density of objects in low earth orbit is high enough that

---

101. For comprehensive information and data see the website of the Organization for the Prohibition of Chemical Weapons, which received the 2013 Nobel Peace Prize for its extensive efforts to eliminate chemical weapons.

102. Remark made at a 1997 speech to the National Space Club. See: http://www.hartford-hwp.com/archives/27c/537.html

attacking some would start a cascade of collisions generating enough space debris to render space exploration, or even the use of satellites infeasible for decades, possibly generations.

The 1967 Outer Space Treaty was reaffirmed in 1999 by 138 nations with only the U.S. and Israel abstaining. It prohibits WMDs in space and the construction of military bases on the moon, but leaves a loophole for conventional, laser and high energy particle beam weapons. The United Nations Committee on Disarmament has struggled for years to get consensus on a treaty banning these weapons, but has been continually blocked by the United States. A weak, non-binding, voluntary Code of Conduct has been proposed but "the U.S. is insisting on a provision in this third version of the Code of Conduct that, while making a voluntary promise to 'refrain from any action which brings about, directly or indirectly, damage, or destruction, of space objects', qualifies that directive with the language 'unless such action is justified.'" "Justification" is based on the right of self-defense that is built into the UN Charter. Such a qualification renders even a voluntary agreement meaningless. A more robust treaty banning all weapons in outer space is a necessary component of an Alternative Global Security System.[103]

ESTABLISH A PEACE ECONOMY

Realign Military Spending

Demilitarizing security as described above will eliminate the need for many weapons programs and military bases, providing an opportunity for government and military-dependent corporations to switch these resources to creating genuine wealth. It can also reduce the tax burden on society and create more jobs. In the U.S., for every $1 billion spent in the military, more than twice the number of jobs at wider spectrum of pay grades would be created if the same amount were spent in the civilian sector.[104] The trade-offs from shifting federal spending priorities with U.S. tax dollars away from the military toward other programs are tremendous.[105]

Spending on a militarized national "defense" is astronomical. The United States alone spends more than the next 15 countries combined on its military.[106]

---

103. A draft sample treaty to achieve this can be seen at the Global Network for the Prohibition of Weapons and Nuclear Power In Space, at http://www.space4peace.org

104. Researchers found that investments in clean energy, healthcare and education create a much larger number of jobs across all pay ranges than spending the same amount of funds with the military. For the complete study see: *The U.S. Employment Effects of Military and Domestic Spending Priorities: 2011 Update* at http://www.peri.umass.edu/fileadmin/pdf/published_study/PERI_military_spending_2011.pdf

105. Try the National Priorities Project's Trade-Offs calculator to see what U.S. tax dollars could have paid for instead of 2015 Department of Defense budget: https://www.nationalpriorities.org/interactive-data/trade-offs/

106. See the Stockholm International Peace Research Institute Military Expenditure Database.

The United States spends $1.3 trillion dollars annually on the Pentagon Budget, nuclear weapons (in the Energy Department budget), veteran's services, the CIA and Homeland Security.[107] The world as a whole spends over $2 trillion. Numbers of this magnitude are hard to grasp. Note that 1 million seconds equals 12 days, 1 billion seconds equals 32 years, and 1 trillion seconds equals 32,000 years. And yet, the highest level of military spending in the world was unable to prevent the 9/11 attacks, halt nuclear proliferation, end terrorism, or suppress resistance to occupations in the Middle East. No matter how much money is spent on war, it does not work.

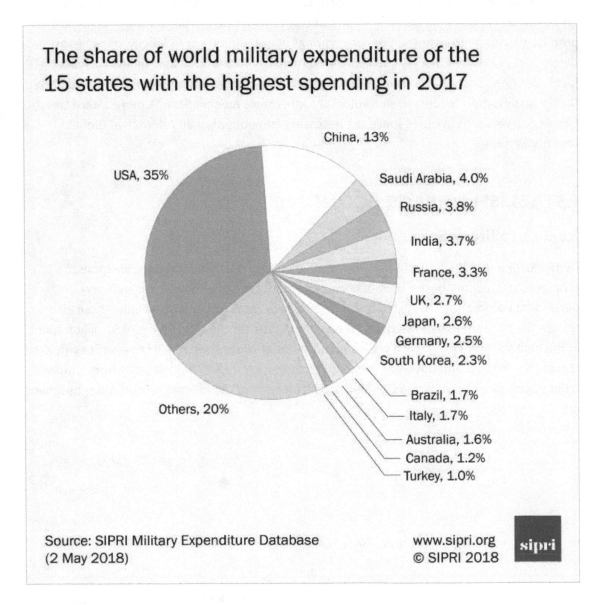

The share of world military expenditure of the 15 states with the highest spending in 2017

China, 13%
USA, 35%
Saudi Arabia, 4.0%
Russia, 3.8%
India, 3.7%
France, 3.3%
UK, 2.7%
Japan, 2.6%
Germany, 2.5%
South Korea, 2.3%
Brazil, 1.7%
Italy, 1.7%
Australia, 1.6%
Canada, 1.2%
Turkey, 1.0%
Others, 20%

Source: SIPRI Military Expenditure Database (2 May 2018)

www.sipri.org
© SIPRI 2018

sipri

---

107. Download the War Resisters League federal spending pie chart at https://www.warresisters.org/sites/default/ files/2015%20pie%20chart%20-%20high%20res.pdf

Military spending is also a serious drain on a nation's economic strength, as pioneering economist Adam Smith pointed out. Smith argued that military spending is economically unproductive. Decades ago, economists commonly used "military burden" almost synonymously with "military budget." Currently, military industries in the U.S. receive more capital investment from the state than all other private industries combined. Transferring this investment capital to the free market sector either directly by grants for conversion or by lowering taxes or paying down the national debt (with its huge annual interest payments) would inject a huge incentive for economic development. A Security System combining the elements described above (and to be described in following sections) would cost a fraction of the present U.S. military budget and would underwrite a process of economic conversion. Furthermore, it would create more jobs. One billion dollars of federal investment in the military creates 11,200 jobs, whereas the same investment in clean energy technology would yield 16,800, in health care 17,200 and in education 26,700.[108]

Economic conversion requires changes in technology, economics and the political process for shifting from military to civilian markets. It is the process of transferring the human and material resources used to make one product to the making of a different one; for example, converting from building missiles to building light rail cars. This type of conversion is feasible: private industry does it all the time. Converting the military industry to making products of use value to society would add to the economic strength of a nation, instead of detracting from it. Resources presently employed in making weapons and maintaining military bases could be redirected to many areas of domestic investment and foreign aid. Infrastructure is always in need of repair and upgrading including transportation infrastructure such as roads, bridges, and rail networks, as well as energy grids, schools, water and sewer systems, and renewable energy installations. Just imagine how the billions spent on militarism could be reallocated to assist cities like Flint, Michigan and Hoosick Falls, New York, where citizens, many of them poor minorities, are poisoned with lead-contaminated water. Another investment area is innovation leading to reindustrialization of economies that are overloaded with low-paying service industries and far too dependent on debt payments and foreign imports of goods, a practice that also adds to the carbon loading of the atmosphere. Airbases, for example, could be converted to affordable housing developments, entrepreneurship incubators, solar-panel factories, or solar panel arrays.

---

108. See: *The U.S. Employment Effects of Military and Domestic Spending Priorities: 2011 Update* at http://www. peri. umass.edu/fileadmin/pdf/published_study/PERI_military_spending_2011.pdf

Meet Study and Action Partner Lindsay Koshgarian: Research Director, National Priorities Project

As Research Director at National Priorities Project (NPP), Lindsay works to show Americans how spending and tax decisions made in Washington affect their lives. She focuses on the inherent trade-offs between military and human development spending. Lindsay is featured in a video on Study War No More introducing a discussion on how we might establish a sustainable global economy as a foundation for peace. Join the discussion and check out Lindsay's video here: http://bit.ly/StudyWarNoMore12

The main obstacles to economic conversion, apart from the corruption of government by money, are the fear of job loss and the need to retrain both labor and management. Jobs will need to be guaranteed by the state while the retraining takes place, or other forms of compensation must be paid to those currently working in the military industry, in order to avoid major unemployment during the transition from a war to a peacetime status.

To be successful, conversion needs to be part of a larger political program of arms reduction. It will require national level meta-planning and financial assistance, as well as intensive local planning as communities with military bases envision transformation and corporations determine what their new niche can be in the free market. This will require tax dollars, but, in the end, will save far more than is invested in redevelopment as states end the economic drain of military spending and replace it with profitable peace time economies creating useful consumer goods.

Attempts have been made to legislate conversion, such as the Nuclear Disarmament and Economic Conversion Act of 1999, which links nuclear disarmament to conversion. A press conference announcing the bill observed:

> "The bill would require the United States to disable and dismantle its nuclear weapons and to refrain from replacing them with weapons of mass destruction once foreign countries possessing nuclear weapons enact and execute similar requirements. The bill also provides that the resources used to sustain our nuclear weapons program be used to address human and infrastructure needs such as housing, health care, education, agriculture, and the environment. So I would see a direct transfer of funds.

Legislation of this sort requires more public support to pass. Success may grow from a smaller scale. The state of Connecticut has created a commission to work on transition. Other states and localities may follow Connecticut's lead. Some momentum for this grew out of a misperception that military spending was being reduced in Washington. We need to either prolong that misperception, make it a reality (obviously the best choice), or persuade local and state governments to take the initiative anyway."[109]

The Economics of War Prevention

The costs of war are obviously too expensive. Dr. Scilla Elworthy developed a compelling "Business Plan to Build a World Without War."[110] Two billion dollars over ten years for peace is not some abstract aspirational goal for humanity, but a sound business plan. These costs dwarf the $ 1,686 billion of estimated global military expenditure every year[111] or the $ 14.3 trillion of global economic impact of violence.[112] The core of the plan evolves around 25 principles on the local, national and global levels, supported by examples and specific implementation plans. Quantifying the cost of alternatives to war in this kind of itemized overview is groundbreaking.

---

109. Transcript of July 30, 1999, Press Conference - HR-2545: "Nuclear Disarmament and Economic Conversion Act of 1999"

110. See her recent book: *The Business Plan for Peace: Building a World Without War.* https://www.scillaelworthy.com/the-business-plan-for-peace/

111. Stockholm International Peace Research Institute - Military Expenditure https://www.sipri.org/research/armament-and-disarmament/arms-transfers-and-military-spending/military-expenditure

112. Institute for Economics and Peace: 2017 Global Peace Index - http://visionofhumanity.org/indexes/global-peace-index/

BASIC STRATEGIES FOR BUILDING PEACE * A BUSINESS PLAN FOR PEACE Dr. Scilla Elworthy[113]

Local Conflict Prevention	National / Regional Conflict Prevention	International Conflict Prevention
Systems the effectively prevent conflict at the local level:	Systems for preventing conflict at national/regional levels:	Systems for preventing conflict at international levels:
• Locally-led peacebuilding	• National infrastructure for peace	• United Nations Emergency Peace Service
• Regional platforms for joined-up approach	• Enable qualified women to fill policy-making roles in peace and security	• Regional mediation
• Breaking cycle of violence through training, consultation and bridge building	• Women countering violent extremism	• Campaign for global brake on arms trading
• Addressing long-term influence and effects of trauma	• Truth and Reconciliation Commissions to break the cycles of violence	• Defuse violent responses to terrorism
	• National budgets for war prevention	• Deprive terrorism of publicity
	• Cut government support for arms trading	• Global Peace Index - top ten to invest
	• Switch production from arms production to renewable energy	• Youth employment in the Middle East
	• Multi-stakeholder dialog	• The Sunni-Shia divide
	• Peace buildings	• Early warning systems that work
		• Early intervention
		• Engage corporate leaders in the business of peace
		• Copy Bhutan's example of Gross National Happiness
Total costs of systems to prevent conflict at local levels (10-year plan) $159,300,000	Total costs of systems to prevent conflict at national/regional levels (10-year plan) $664,450,000	Total cost of systems for preventing conflict at international levels (10-year plan) $1,178,125,000

Create a Stable, Fair and Sustainable Global Economy

War and economic and environmental injustice are tied together in many ways, not the least of which is high youth unemployment in volatile regions, such as the Middle East, where it creates a seed bed for growing extremists. And the global, oil-based economy is an obvious cause of militarized conflict and imperial ambitions to project power and protect U.S. access to foreign resources. The imbalance between the affluent northern economies and the poverty of the global south can be righted by a Global Aid Plan that takes into account the need to conserve ecosystems upon which economies rest, and to democratize the international economic institutions including the World Trade Organization, the International Monetary Fund and the International Bank for Reconstruction and Development.

---

113. These strategies form the basis for Elworthy's business plan for peace. In her book, she itemizes and budgets these strategies over 10 years.

A Global Security System: An Alternative to War 2018-19 Edition

On Divestment

Models for various kinds of divestment campaigns have been and are being developed around fossil fuels, nuclear weapons, and the Israeli occupation of Palestine. There may be new opportunities to advance nuclear divestment as the new treaty banning nuclear weapons possession comes into being. A key step toward abolishing all war will be divestment from all weapons of war. World BEYOND War has initiated campaigns to divest public (government) dollars from the biggest war profiteers.

While governments buy weapons, market weapons to other governments, donate weapons to other governments, and bestow tax breaks on weapons dealers, there is another less-visible way in which public money sustains weapons dealing. Public pension and retirement funds are invested, directly and indirectly, in weapons companies. Teachers and other public servants whose interests ought to lie with promoting human needs have their retirement security tied up with maintaining or enlarging the war industry.

Key to divesting this funding are research and lobbying - with lobbying understood to mean all forms of public education and nonviolent activism. A hub for World BEYOND War's work on this is found at:

http://worldbeyondwar.org/divest

There is no polite way to say that business is destroying the world.
- Paul Hawken (Environmentalist, Author)

Political economist Lloyd Dumas states that "a militarized economy distorts and ultimately weakens society". He outlines the basic principles of a peacekeeping economy.[114] These are:

- Establish balanced relationships – everyone gains benefit at least equal to their contribution and there is little incentive to disrupt the relationship. Example: The European Union – they debate, there are conflicts, but there are no threats of war within the EU.

- Emphasize development – Most of the wars since WWII have been fought in developing countries. Poverty and missing opportunities are breeding grounds for violence.

---

114. Dumas, L. J. (2011). *The peacekeeping economy: Using economic relationships to build a more peaceful, prosperous, and secure world.* New Haven, CT: Yale University Press.

Development is an effective counter-terrorism strategy, as it weakens the support network for terrorist groups, which often recruit young, uneducated males in urban areas.[115]

- Minimize ecological stress – The competition for non-renewable resources ("stress-generating resources") – most notably oil and water – generates dangerous conflicts between nations and groups within nations.

It is proven that war is more likely to happen where there is oil.[116] Using natural resources more efficiently, developing and using non-polluting technologies and procedures, and shifting toward qualitative rather than quantitative economic growth can reduce ecological stress.

Democratize International Economic Institutions (WTO, IMF, IBRD)

The global economy is administered, financed and regulated by three institutions – The World Trade Organization (WTO), The International Monetary Fund (IMF), and the International Bank for Reconstruction and Development (IBRD; "World Bank"[117]). The problem with these bodies is that they are typically undemocratic and favor the rich nations against the poorer nations, unduly restrict environmental and labor protections, and lack transparency, discourage sustainability, and encourage resource extraction and dependence.[118] The unelected and unaccountable governing board of the WTO can override the labor and environmental laws of nations, rendering the populace vulnerable to exploitation and environmental degradation with its various health implications.

---

115. Supported by the following study: Mousseau, Michael. "Urban Poverty and Support for Islamist Terror Survey Results of Muslims in Fourteen Countries." Journal of Peace Research 48, no. 1 (January 1, 2011): 35–47. This assertion should not be confused with an overly simplistic interpretation of the multiple root causes of terrorism.

116. Supported by the following study: Bove, V., Gleditsch, K. S., & Sekeris, P. G. (2015). "Oil above Water" Economic Interdependence and Third-party Intervention. Journal of Conflict Resolution. Key findings are: Foreign governments are 100 times more likely to intervene in civil wars when the country at war has large oil reserves. Oil-dependent economies have favored stability and support dictators rather than emphasizing democracy.

117. It has been pointed out by some of our readers, amongst them former World Bank employees, that its structural adjustment lending programs of the past do not depict an accurate picture regarding the present-day World Bank. The history and harmful effects of structural adjustment programs, which tightened the belt around the thin waists of poor countries, are not to be discounted. However, in assessing current World Bank operations, it stands to reason to give credit for clear development successes, which are very significant, while taking the Bank to task and holding it accountable for cases of shortcomings in its lending processes or poorly conceived and executed projects. Recent World Bank efforts have encouraged greater civil society participation, including participation of NGOs in more than half of the Bank's projects. Emphases on sustainable development and eradicating extreme poverty have shifted strategies towards growing economies in an inclusive, labor-intensive way; invest in the human capital of people; and insure poor and vulnerable people against shocks. Read more on the World Bank's poverty initiatives here: http://www.worldbank.org/en/topic/poverty/overview#1

118. For some, the underlying assumptions of the economic theory need to be questioned. For example, the organization Positive Money (http://positivemoney.org/) aims to build a movement for a fair, democratic and sustainable money system by taking the power to create money away from the banks and return it to a democratic and accountable process, by creating money free of debt, and by putting new money into the real economy rather than financial markets and property bubbles.

"The current form of corporate-dominated globalization is escalating the plunder of the earth's riches, increasing the exploitation of workers, expanding police and military repression and leaving poverty in its wake".
- Sharon Delgado (Author, Director Earth Justice Ministries)

Globalization itself is not the issue—it's free trade. The complex of government elites and transnational corporations that control these institutions are driven by an ideology of Market Fundamentalism, or "Free Trade," a euphemism for one-sided trade in which wealth flows from the poor to the rich. The legal and financial systems that these institutions create and enforce allow for the export of industry to havens of pollution in countries that oppress workers who attempt to organize for decent wages, health, safety and environmental protections. The manufactured goods are exported back to the developed countries as consumer goods. The costs are externalized to the poor and the global environment. As the less developed nations have gone deeply into debt under this regime, they are required to accept IMF "austerity plans," which destroy their social safety nets, creating a class of powerless, impoverished workers for the northern-owned factories. The regime also impacts agriculture. Fields that ought to be growing food for people are instead growing flowers for the cut-flower trade in Europe and the U.S. Or they have been taken over by elites, the subsistence farmers shoved out, and they grow corn or raise cattle for export to the global north. The poor drift into the mega-cities where, if lucky, they find work in the oppressive factories creating export goods. The injustice of this regime creates resentment and leads to, oftentimes violent, revolution, which in turn results in police and military repression by the state. The police and military are often trained in crowd suppression by the United States military at the "Western Hemisphere Institute for Security Cooperation" (formerly "School of the Americas"). At this institution, training includes advanced combat arms, psychological operations, military intelligence and commando tactics.[119] All of this is destabilizing and creates more insecurity in the world.

The solution requires policy changes and a moral awakening in the global north. The obvious first move is to cease training police and military for dictatorial regimes. Second, the governing boards of these international financial institutions need to be democratized. They are now dominated by the Industrial North nations. Third, so-called "free trade" policies need to be replaced with fair trade policies. All of this requires a moral shift, from cheap consumerism to a sense of global solidarity and a realization that damage to ecosystems anywhere has planetary implications, most obviously in terms of climate change, and a resulting climate refugee crisis, leading to militarizing borders. If people can be assured of a decent life in their own countries, they will not be likely to try to immigrate illegally.

---

119. For more information see School of the Americas Watch at: www.soaw.org

Create an Environmentally Sustainable Global Aid Plan

Development reinforces diplomacy and defense, reducing long-term threats to
our national security by helping build stable, prosperous and peaceful societies.
- 2006 United States National Security Strategy Plan

A related solution to democratizing the international economic institutions is to institute a Global Aid Plan to achieve stabilizing economic and environmental justice worldwide.[120] The goals would be similar to the UN Millennium Development Goals to end poverty and hunger, develop local food security, provide education and health care, and to achieve these goals by creating stable, efficient, sustainable economic development that does not exacerbate climate shift. It will also need to provide funds to assist with the resettlement of climate refugees. The Plan would be administered by a new, international non-governmental organization to prevent it from becoming a foreign policy tool of rich nations. It would be funded by a dedication of 2-5 percent of GDP from the advanced industrial nations for twenty years. For the U.S. this amount would be approximately a few hundred billion dollars, far less than is the $1.3 trillion currently spent on the failed national security system. The plan would be administered at ground level by an International Peace and Justice Corps made up of volunteers. It would require strict accounting and transparency from the recipient governments to ensure that the aid actually got to the people.

RECONFIGURE THE RESPONSE TO TERRORISM

Following the 9/11 attacks on the World Trade Center, the U.S. attacked terrorist bases in Afghanistan, initiating a long, unsuccessful war. Adopting a military approach has not only failed to end terrorism, it has resulted in the erosion of constitutional liberties, the commission of human rights abuses and violations of international law, and has provided cover for dictators and democratic governments to further abuse their powers, justifying abuses in the name of "fighting terrorism."

The terrorist threat to people in the Western world has been exaggerated and there has been an overreaction in the media, public and political realm.[121] Many benefit from exploiting the threat of terrorism in what now can be called a homeland-security-industrial complex. As Glenn Greenwald writes:

---

120. Somewhat similar, the so-called Marshall Plan was a post-World War II American economic initiative to help rebuild European economies. See more at: https://en.wikipedia.org/wiki/Marshall_Plan

121. The following are only some of the analyses dealing with the exaggerated terrorism threats: Lisa Stampnitzky's Disciplining Terror. How Experts Invented 'Terrorism'; Stephen Walt's What terrorist threat?; John Mueller and Mark Stewart's The Terrorism Delusion. America's Overwrought Response to September 11

"…the private and public entities that shape government policy and drive political discourse profit far too much in numerous ways to allow rational considerations of the Terror threat."
- Glenn Greenwald[122]

Research shows that military action is often an ineffective and counterproductive tool for countering terrorism, as it fuels grievances of already marginalized communities, feeding into narratives employed by terrorist groups and providing these groups with new recruits.[123] Moreover, both deployment of troops and weapons exports to another country increase the chance of attacks from terror organizations from that country.[124]

"The world's most powerful military did nothing to prevent or stop the 9-11 attacks. Virtually every terrorist caught, every terrorist plot foiled has been the result of first-rate intelligence and police work, not the threat or use of military force. Military force has also been useless in preventing the spread of weapons of mass destruction."
- Lloyd J. Dumas (Professor of Political Economy)

To better understand and address terrorist violence, it is necessary to analyze terrorism as a tool (like other forms of political violence) for pursuing interests in a broader conflict context and to view security/insecurity from the perspectives of those most marginalized in society.[125] In general, a more effective strategy would be to treat terrorist attacks as crimes against humanity, instead of acts of war, and to use all the resources of the international police community to bring perpetrators to justice before the International Criminal Court. It is notable that an incredibly powerful military was unable to prevent the worst attacks on the U.S. since Pearl Harbor.

A professional field of peace and conflict studies scholars and practitioners is continuously providing responses to terrorism, which are superior to the so-called experts of the terrorism

---

122. See Glenn Greenwald, The sham "terrorism" expert industry at http://www.salon.com/2012/08/15/the_sham_terrorism_expert_industry/

123. Counterproductive Effects of Military Counterterrorism Strategies: http://communication.warpreventioninitiative.org/counterproductive-effects-military-counterterrorism-strategies

124. "Military Support and an Increased Vulnerability to Terrorist Attacks" - http://communication.warpreventioninitiative.org/military-support-and-an-increased-vulnerability-to-terrorist-attacks/

125. "Counterproductive Effects of Military Counterterrorism Strategies" at http://communication.warpreventioninitiative.org/counterproductive-effects-military-counterterrorism-strategies/

industry. Just consider this list of nonviolent tactics, developed by peace scholar Tom Hastings:[126]

Immediate Nonviolent Responses to Terrorism

- "Smart" sanctions that focus on and affect elites only

- Mediation, negotiation

- Adjudication

- International law enforcement

- Nonviolent resistance to any violence

- Interposition

- Global opprobrium for all violence

Long-Term Nonviolent Responses to Terrorism

- Stop and reverse all arms trade and manufacture

- Consumption reduction by rich nations

- Massive aid to poor nations and populations

- Refugee repatriation or emigration

- Debt relief to poorest nations

- Education about roots of terrorism

- Education and training about nonviolent power

- Promote culturally and ecologically sensitive tourism and cultural exchanges

- Build sustainable and just economy, energy use and distribution, agriculture

If we don't use these alternatives, it is not because they are unavailable, but because of artificially imposed constraints, lack of interest, or self-interest. While these solutions are not magical, they do work. We have to look at them in terms of effectiveness versus the military intervention. And it is beyond doubt that they are more effective as short, medium, and long-term responses.

If we examine the case of ISIS, there are many constructive nonviolent alternatives that could be pursued, which should not be mistaken for inaction. These include: an arms embargo, support of Syrian civil society, support of nonviolent civil resistance[127], pursuit of meaningful

---

126. All responses are thoroughly examined in: Hastings, Tom H. 2004. Nonviolent Responses to Terrorism.

127. See Maria Stephan, *Defeating ISIS Through Civil Resistance? Striking Nonviolently at Sources of Power Could Support Effective Solutions* at http://www.usip.org/olivebranch/2016/07/11/defeating-isis-through-civil-resistance or at http://communication.warpreventioninitiative.org/defeating-isis-with-nonviolent-resistance/

diplomacy with all actors, economic sanctions on ISIS and supporters, closing the border to cut off the sale of oil from ISIS controlled territories and stop the flow of fighters, and humanitarian aid. Long-term strong steps would be the withdrawal of U.S. troops from the region and ending oil imports from the region in order to dissolve terrorism at its roots.[128]

THE ROLE OF WOMEN IN PEACE AND SECURITY

The role of women in peace and security has not been given the appropriate attention. Take, for example, treaties, in particular peace agreements, which are most commonly negotiated and signed in a male-dominated context, by state and non-state armed actors. This context utterly misses the reality on the ground. The "Better Peace Tool" by the International Civil Society Action Network was developed as a guide to inclusive peace processes and negotiations.[129] Women, according to the report, share a vision of societies rooted in social justice and equality; are an important source of practical experience about life in a war zone; and better understand on-the-ground realities. Peace processes therefore should not be narrowly focused security or political ones, but inclusive societal processes. This is what is called the democratization of peacemaking.

Photo: The Colombian Ombudsman Office. *source: http://www.swemfa.se/2017/09/20/morewomenmorepeace-women-peacebuilders-in-colombia/. Women peacebuilders in Colombia.

"No women, no peace" - this headline described the central role of women and gender equality in the peace deal between the Colombian government and the FARC rebel group, marking the end of a 50-plus-year civil war in August of 2016. The substance and the processes of the peace accord reflect the contributions of women. A gender sub-commission ensured line-by-line that women's and LGBT's perspectives were considered.[130]

---

128. Comprehensive discussions outlining viable, nonviolent alternatives to the ISIS threat can be found at http://worldbeyondwar.org/new-war-forever-war-world-beyond-war/ and http://warpreventioninitiative.org/images/PDF/ISIS_matrix_report.pdf

129. http://www.betterpeacetool.org

130. No women, no peace. Colombian women made sure gender equality was at the center of a groundbreaking peace deal with the FARC (http://qz.com/768092/colombian-women-made-sure-gender-

Hard evidence and field experience have shown:

*"A gender perspective can help identify strategic blind spots for peace and
stability operations". - Sahana Dharmapuri (Director, Our Secure Future
Program - One Earth Future Foundation)*

There are numerous examples of creative and determined women peace activists in
the secular and faith-based realms. Sister Joan Chittister has been a leading voice for
women, peace, and justice for decades. Iranian Nobel Peace Prize Laureate Shirin Ebadi
is an outspoken advocate against nuclear weapons. Worldwide, indigenous women are
increasingly recognized as powerful agents of social change. A less known, but nonetheless
wonderful, example is the Young Women's Peace Charter aimed at building commitment
and understanding of the challenges and obstacles faced by young women in conflict-
affected countries, as well as other societies within the framework of the Young Women's
Peace Academy.[131] The Charter aims to spread feminism worldwide, eliminate patriarchal
structures, and secure the safety for feminists, women peacebuilders and human rights
defenders. The goals are accompanied by a powerful set of recommendations which can act
as a model for women in many contexts.

Further examples abound. Women played a particular role in peace talks in Guatemala
in the 1990s. An alliance of women coordinated peacebuilding activities in Somalia. In
Northern Ireland, women led a political movement to enhance women's power and influence
the peace agreement and peace processes there. And women are helping to forge cross-
community efforts in the ongoing Israeli-Palestinian conflict.[132] In general, women's voices
help to advance alternative agendas from those usually presented by leaders in power.[133]

Giving representatives from the entire community a voice in peace and reconciliation
processes after an armed conflict is essential for achieving long-term peace. In most cases,
however, half of the population is routinely excluded from this process. When women
are excluded from peace processes, the experiences, knowledge and needs of half of the
population are lost before the country's efforts to rebuild have even begun.[134]

---

equality-was-at-thecenter-of-a-groundbreaking-peace-deal-with-the-farc/)

131. http://kvinnatillkvinna.se/en/files/qbank/6f221fcb5c504fe96789df252123770b.pdf

132. Ramsbotham, O., Miall, H., & Woodhouse, T. (2016). Contemporary conflict resolution: The prevention,
management and transformation of deadly conflicts. 4th ed. Cambridge: Polity.

133. See "Women, Religion, and Peace" in Zelizer, C. (2013). Integrated peacebuilding: Innovative approaches to
transforming conflict. Boulder, CO: Westview Press.

134. More women in peace processes at http://kvinnatillkvinna.se/en/what-we-do/more-women-in-peace-
processes/

Acknowledging the existing gap in the role of women and peacebuilding, advances have been made. Most notably at the policy level, UNSCR 1325 (2000) provides a "global framework for mainstreaming gender in all peace processes, including peacekeeping, peacebuilding, and post conflict reconstruction."[135] At the same time, it is clear that policies and rhetorical commitments are only a first step toward changing a male-dominated paradigm.

In creating a World BEYOND War, a gender-sensitive approach to our thinking and acting needs to be adopted. The following stages of engendering war prevention are required:[136]

- Making women visible as agents of change in preventing war and building peace

- Removing male bias in war prevention and peacebuilding data collection and research

- Rethinking drivers of war and peace to take gender into account

- Incorporating and mainstreaming gender into policy-making and practice

Meet Study and Action Partner Mavic Cabrera Balleza: Founder, Global Network of Women Peacebuilders

Founder and International Coordinator of the Global Network of Women Peacebuilders (GNWP), Mavic initiated the Philippine national action planning process on UN Security Council Resolution 1325 on Women, Peace and Security. She also served as the international consultant to Nepal's National Action Plan and has provided technical support in 1325 national action planning to Georgia, Guatemala, Japan, Jordan and South Sudan. GNWP has been pioneering the Localization of UNSCR 1325 and 1820 program that is regarded as a best practice example and is now implemented in 11 countries. Mavic is featured in a video on Study War No More introducing a discussion on involving women in peace and security decision making. Join the discussion and check out Mavic's video here: http://bit.ly/StudyWarNoMore13video

---

135. Zelizer (2013), p. 110

136. These points are modified from "the four stages of engendering conflict resolution" by Ramsbotham, O., Miall, H., & Woodhouse, T. (2016). *Contemporary conflict resolution: The prevention, management and transformation of deadly conflicts.* 4th ed. Cambridge: Polity.

MANAGING CONFLICT WITHOUT VIOLENCE

EXECUTIVE SUMMARY

This component of our global security system comprises the tools and institutions necessary for assuring security and managing conflict nonviolently. Our strategy here seeks a balance between reforming existing institutions and establishing new ones. We acknowledge the weaknesses inherent in the United Nations system, especially its emphasis on collective security and the challenges of overcoming national self-interest. While these are tremendous, essentially deal-breaking obstacles, the UN is currently our primary form of global governance. At the same time, many functions of the UN, especially outside the security decision making bodies, provide hope. Thus, our strategy carefully considers several reforms to strengthen UN security functions. International law provides another key function in our system. While limited in enforceability within an anarchic nation state system, international law is an essential nonviolent tool for managing disputes and conflicts. To strengthen international law, we propose a handful of reforms to improve the International Criminal Court (ICC) and the International Court of Justice (ICJ); explore possibilities for enforcing existing treaties and creating new ones; and recommend the establishment of truth and reconciliation commissions and other alternative justice / peacebuilding approaches. We also firmly acknowledge the limited functioning of a system comprised of nation states and identify strategies for greater participation of civil society in the functioning of our security system. Several civilian peacekeeping forces are already serving vital roles in managing conflict in zones of violence around the world. We also consider the potential of Gene Sharp's vision of establishing Civilian-Based Defense Forces (CBD). CBD is a bold, nonviolent alternative that can make invading a country very unappealing. It also supports a cultural shift in thinking about security and would require training all citizens in strategic nonviolent methods of resistance. Finally, we propose a few alternatives to current approaches to global governance and invite future citizens to consider the essential principles and functions that should guide a peaceful world order.

STRATEGIC POLICY AND ACTION RECOMMENDATIONS

- Demand further study of United Nations reforms supporting a paradigm shift from collective to common security.

- Pursue democratic changes to UN Security Council composition and permanent member veto.

- Develop better conflict forecasting and management tools.

- Establish rapid response peacekeeping and peacebuilding teams.

- Increase UN funding commensurate with current military funding.

- Strengthen enforceability and increase compliance to international law.

- Increase the role of global civil society in peace and security decision making and action.

- Study, explore feasibility, model and design large scale training for Civilian-Based Defense (CBD).

- Explore and model new proposals for humane global governance.

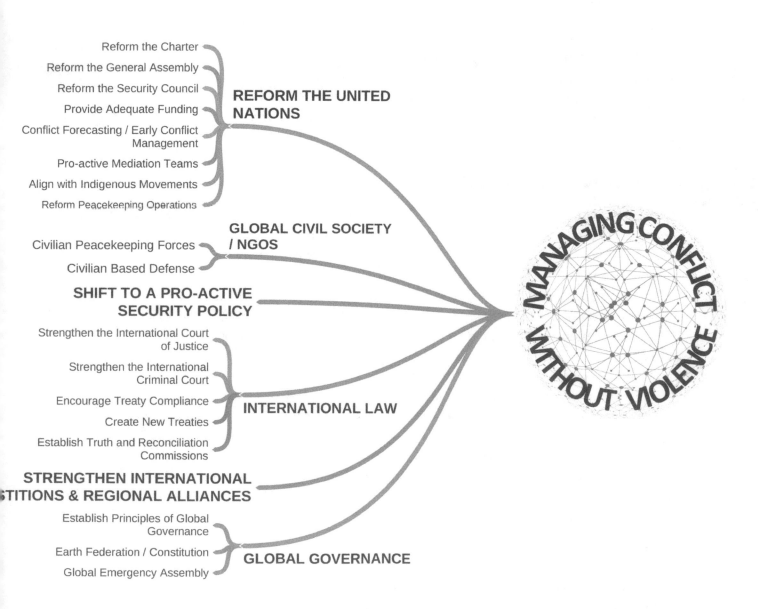

The reactionary approaches and established institutions for managing international and civil conflicts have proven to be insufficient and often inadequate. We propose a series of improvements.

SHIFTING TO A PRO-ACTIVE POSTURE

Dismantling the institutions of the War System and the beliefs and attitudes that underlie it will not be enough. An Alternative Global Security System needs to be constructed. Much of this system is already in place, having evolved over the past hundred years, although either in embryonic form or in great need of strengthening. Some of it exists only in ideas that need to be institutionalized.

The existing parts of the system should not be seen as the static end-products of a peaceful world, but as elements of dynamic, imperfect processes of human evolution, which leads to an increasingly nonviolent world with more equality for everyone. Only a proactive posture will help strengthen the Alternative Global Security System.

STRENGTHENING INTERNATIONAL INSTITUTIONS AND REGIONAL ALLIANCES

International institutions for managing conflict without violence have been evolving for a long time. A body of very functional international law has been developing for centuries and needs to be further developed to be an effective part of a peace system. In 1899 the International Court of Justice (ICJ; the "World Court") was set up to adjudicate disputes between nation states. The League of Nations followed in 1920. An association of 58 sovereign States, the League was based on the principle of collective security, that is, if a State committed aggression, the other states would either enact economic sanctions against that State or, as a "last resort" approach, provide military forces to defeat it. The League did settle some minor disputes and initiated global-level peace building efforts. The problem was that the member states failed, in the main, to do what they said they would do, and so the aggressions of Japan, Italy, and Germany were not prevented, leading to World War II, the most destructive war in history. It is also noteworthy that the U.S. refused to join. After the Allied victory, the United Nations was set up as a new attempt at collective security. Also an association of sovereign states, the UN was supposed to resolve disputes and, where that was not feasible, the Security Council could decide to enact sanctions or provide a counter military force to deal with an aggressor state.

To-date, sanctions are not without controversy. If badly designed - willingly or unwillingly - they harm innocent people and thus lose legitimacy and support.[137] Those sanctions should be criticized and challenged, so they will be abandoned. At the same time, it is important to recognize how sanctions can be coercive nonviolent methods to handling disputes and

---

137. What Happened to Smart Sanctions? - https://davidcortright.net/2012/11/05/ what-happened-to-smart-sanctions/

preventing wars. Peace science informs us that sanctions can lead countries to diplomatic negotiations, which in turn contribute to future cooperation. Sanctioning governments convey strength and solidarity through shared condemnation.[138] Sanctions need to be "smart" and focus on and affect elites only.

The UN also greatly expanded the peacebuilding initiatives begun by the League. However, the UN was hobbled by built-in structural constraints, and the Cold War between the U.S. and the U.S.S.R. made meaningful cooperation difficult. The two superpowers also set up traditional military alliance systems aimed at one another, NATO and the Warsaw Pact.

Other regional alliance systems were also established. The European Union has kept a peaceful Europe despite differences, the African Union is keeping the peace between Egypt and Ethiopia, and the Association of South-East Asian Nations and the Union de Naciones Suramericanas are developing potential for its members and would-be members toward peace.

While international institutions for managing inter-state conflicts are a vital part of a peace system, the problems with both the League and the UN arose in part from a failure to dismantle the War System. They were set up within it and by themselves were unable to control war or arms races. Some analysts believe that the crux of the problem is that these types of institutions are, in the end, associations of sovereign states, each of which has its own agenda and national priorities, and is not opposed to using war to protect its interests. However, there are many ways that the UN as well as other international institutions can be constructively reformed to become more effective in keeping the peace, including reforms of the Security Council, the General Assembly, peacekeeping forces and actions, funding, its relationship to non-government organizations and the addition of new functions.

REFORM THE UNITED NATIONS

The United Nations was created as a response to World War II to prevent war by negotiation, sanctions, and collective security. The Preamble to the Charter provides the overall mission:

> To save succeeding generations from the scourge of war, which twice in our lifetime has brought untold sorrow to mankind, and to reaffirm faith in fundamental human rights, in the dignity and worth of the human person, in the equal rights of men and women and of nations large and small, and to establish conditions under which justice and respect for the obligations arising from treaties and other sources of international law can be maintained, and to promote social progress and better standards of life in larger freedom...

Reforming the United Nations can and needs to take place at different levels.

---

138. Sanctions as a tool for peace - http://communication.warpreventioninitiative.org/ sanctions-as-a-tool-for-peace/

Reform the Charter to More Effectively Deal with Aggression

The United Nations Charter does not outlaw war; it outlaws aggression. While the Charter does enable the Security Council to take action in response to aggression, it does not provide a blanket justification for interventionism. In fact, nothing in the Charter mandates the UN to take action, and it does require the conflicting parties to first try to settle the dispute themselves by arbitration and next by action of any regional security system to which they belong. Only then is it up to the UN Security Council, which is often rendered impotent by the veto provision (see section below on reforming the Security Council).

The UN Charter does not prohibit States from taking their own action in self-defense. Article 51 reads:

> Nothing in the present Charter shall impair the inherent right of individual or collective self-defence if an armed attack occurs against a Member of the United Nations, until the Security Council has taken measures necessary to maintain international peace and security. Measures taken by Members in the exercise of this right of self-defence shall be immediately reported to the Security Council and shall not in any way affect the authority and responsibility of the Security Council under the present Charter to take at any time such action as it deems necessary in order to maintain or restore international peace and security.

As desirable as it would be to outlaw all forms of warfare, including making war in self-defense, it is hard to see how that can be achieved until a fully developed peace system is in place. However, much progress can be made by changing the Charter to require the Security Council to address all cases of violent conflict immediately upon their commencement by providing a clear course of action to: halt hostilities by means of a ceasefire , require mediation at the UN (with the aid of regional partners if desired), and, if necessary, refer the dispute to the International Court of Justice. This will require several further reforms as listed below, including dealing with the veto, shifting to nonviolent methods as the primary tools by making use of nonviolent unarmed civilian peaceworkers, and providing an adequate (and adequately accountable) police power to enforce its decisions when needed.

It should be added that most wars in recent decades have been illegal under the UN Charter. However, there has been little awareness and no consequences for that fact.

Reform the General Assembly

The General Assembly (GA) is the most democratic of the UN bodies since it includes all the member States. It is concerned primarily with crucial peacebuilding programs. Former Secretary General Kofi Annan suggested that the GA simplify its programs, abandon reliance on consensus since it results in watered-down resolutions, and adopt a supermajority for decision making. The GA needs to pay more attention to implementation and compliance with its decisions. It also needs a more efficient committee system and to involve civil society, that is, NGOs, more directly in its work. Another problem with the GA is that each member State has an equal vote, meaning that a tiny nation with 200,000 citizens has as much weight in voting as a large country like China or India.

Photo: The United Nations as an example of global collaboration through supranational institutions.

A reform idea gaining popularity is to add to the GA a Parliamentary Assembly of members elected by the citizens of each country and in which the number of seats allocated to each country would more accurately reflect population and thus be more democratic. Then any decisions of the GA would have to pass both houses. Such "global MPs" would also be able to represent the common welfare of humanity in general rather than being required to follow the dictates of their governments back home as the current State ambassadors are.

Reform the Security Council

Article 42 of the Charter gives the Security Council the responsibility for maintaining and restoring the peace. It is the only UN body with binding authority on member States. The Council does not have an armed force to carry out its decisions; rather, it has binding authority to call on the armed forces of member States. However, the composition and methods of the Security Council are antiquated and only minimally effective in keeping or restoring the peace.

Composition

The Council is composed of 15 members, 5 of whom are permanent. These are the victorious powers in World War II (U.S., Russia, U.K., France, and China). They are also the members who have veto power. At the time of writing the Charter in 1945, they demanded these conditions, or would not have permitted the UN to come into being. These permanent five also claim and possess leading seats on the governing bodies of the major committees of the UN, giving them a disproportionate and undemocratic amount of influence. They are also, along with Germany, the major arms dealers to the world.

The world has changed dramatically in the intervening decades. The UN has gone from 50 members to 193, and population balances have changed dramatically as well. Further, the way in which Security Council seats are allotted by 4 regions is also unrepresentative, with Europe and the UK having 4 seats, while Latin America only has 1. Africa is also underrepresented. It is only rarely that a Muslim nation is represented on the Council. It is long past time to rectify this situation if the UN wants to command respect in these regions.

One proposal is to increase the number of electoral regions to 9 in which each would have one permanent member and each region have 2 revolving members to add up to a Council of 27 seats, thus more perfectly reflecting national, cultural and population realities.

Also, the nature of the threats to peace and security has changed dramatically. At the time of the founding the current arrangement might have made sense given the need for great power agreement and that the main threat to peace and security was seen to be armed aggression. While armed aggression and militarism is still an extreme threat – and permanent member the United States the worst recidivist – great military power is just one threat amongst many such as global warming, mass movements of peoples, global disease threats, the arms trade and criminality.

Revise or Eliminate the Veto

The Security Council's veto is exercised over four types of decisions: the use of force to maintain or restore the peace, appointments to the Secretary-General's position, applications for UN membership, and amending the Charter and procedural matters, which can prevent questions from even coming to the floor. Also, in the other bodies, the Permanent 5 tend to exercise a de facto veto. In Council, the veto has been used 265 times, primarily by the U.S. and the former Soviet Union, to block action, often rendering the UN impotent.

The veto hamstrings the Security Council. It is profoundly unfair in that it enables the holders to prevent any action against their own violations of the Charter's prohibition on aggression. It is also used as a favor in shielding their client states' misdeeds from Security Council actions. One proposal is to simply discard the veto. Another is to allow permanent members to cast a veto but to make three members casting it necessary to block passage of a substantive issue. Procedural issues should not be subject to the veto.

Other Necessary Reforms of the Security Council

Three procedures need to be added. Currently nothing requires the Security Council to act. At a minimum, the Council should be required to take up all issues that threaten peace and security, and decide whether to act on them or not ("The Duty to Decide"). Second is "The Requirement for Transparency." The Council should be required to disclose its reasons for deciding, or not, to take up the issue of a conflict. Further, the Council meets in secret about 98 percent of the time. At the least, its substantive deliberations need to be transparent. Third, the "Duty to Consult" would require the Council to take reasonable measures to consult with nations that would be impacted by its decisions.

Provide Adequate Funding

The UN's "Regular Budget" funds the General Assembly, Security Council, Economic and Social Council, the International Court of Justice, and special missions, such as the UN Assistance Mission to Afghanistan. The Peacekeeping Budget is separate. Member states are assessed for both, rates depending on their GDP. The UN also receives voluntary donations, which are about equal to the revenue from assessed funds.

Given its mission, the United Nations is grossly underfunded. The regular two-year budget for 2018 and 2019 is set at $5.4 billion (a 5% reduction from the 2016-17 budget) and the Peacekeeping Budget for the fiscal year 2017-2018 is $6.8 billion, the total amounting to less than one half of one percent of global military expenditures (and less than one percent of U.S. annual military related expenditures). Several proposals have been advanced to adequately fund the UN including a tax of a fraction of one percent on international financial transactions, which could raise up to $300 billion to be applied primarily to UN development and environmental programs, such as reducing child mortality, fighting epidemic diseases such as Ebola, and countering the negative effects of climate change.

Forecasting and Managing Conflicts Early On

Using the Blue Helmets, the UN is already stretched thin to fund 16 peacekeeping missions around the world, putting out or dampening fires that could spread regionally or even globally. While it is, at least in some cases, doing a good job under very difficult conditions, the UN needs to become far more proactive in foreseeing and preventing conflicts where possible, and quickly and nonviolently intervening in conflicts that have ignited in order to put out the fires quickly.

Forecasting

Maintain a permanent expert agency to monitor potential conflicts around the world and recommend immediate action to the Security Council or the Secretary General, beginning with:

Pro-active Mediation Teams

Maintain a permanent set of mediation experts qualified in language and cultural diversity and the latest techniques of non-adversarial mediation to be dispatched rapidly to states where either international aggression or civil war looks imminent. This has started with the so-called Standby Team of Mediation Experts who act as on-call advisers to peace envoys around the world on issues such as mediation strategy, power-sharing, constitution-making, human rights and natural resources.[139]

Align Early with Indigenous Nonviolent Movements

To date, the UN has shown little understanding of the power that nonviolent movements within countries can exercise to prevent civil conflicts from becoming violent civil wars. At the least, the UN needs to be able to assist these movements by pressuring governments to avoid violent reprisals against them, while bringing UN mediation teams to bear. The UN needs to engage with these movements. When engagement with movements is deemed difficult due to concerns about infringing on national sovereignty, the UN can do the following.

---

139. See http://www.un.org/en/peacekeeping/operations/current.shtml for current peacekeeping missions

Reform Peacekeeping Operations

The current UN Peacekeeping operations have major problems, including conflicting rules of engagement, lack of interaction with affected communities, lack of women representation, gender-based violence and failure to deal with the changing nature of warfare. A UN High-Level Independent Panel of Peace Operations, chaired by Nobel Peace Laureate Jose Ramos-Horta, recommended 4 essential shifts to UN peace operations:

1. Primacy of politics: political solutions must guide all UN peace operations.

2. Responsive operations: missions should be tailored to context and include the full spectrum of responses.

3. Stronger partnerships: developing resilient global and local peace and security architectures,

4. Field-focused and people-centered: a renewed resolve to serve and protect the people.[140]

According to Mel Duncan, co-founder of the Nonviolent Peaceforce, the panel also recognized that civilians can and do play an important role in the direct protection of civilians.

Even after the suggested improvements, the Blue Helmets peacekeeping operations should be used as a last resort, after mediation and other proactive measures, within a more democratically reformed UN structure. Even with those considerations, the greater militarization partiality entailed by so-called robust peacekeeping, may actually put civilians at risk, along with peacekeepers, other UN officials, and independent humanitarian actors; and in some cases also diminish humanitarian space/access.[141]

To be clear, the operations of UN Peacekeeping or civilian protection forces are not what one would consider a military intervention for the sake of peace and security. The fundamental mission of international peacekeeping, policing, or civilian protection authorized by the United Nations or another international body is different from military intervention. A military intervention is the introduction of outside military forces into an existing conflict through the use of arms, air strikes and combat troops in order to influence a military outcome and defeat an enemy. It is the use of deadly force on a massive scale. UN Peacekeeping, on the other hand, is guided by three basic principles: (1) consent of the parties; (2) impartiality; and (3) non-use of force except in self-defense and defense of the mandate. Despite these principles, civilian protection is being falsely used as a disguise for military interventions with less noble motives. The human costs never justify any form of military intervention, even if long-term improvements are stated.[142]

---

140. The Global Peace Operations Review is a web-portal providing analysis and data on peacekeeping operations and political missions. See the website at: http://peaceoperationsreview.org

141. "The Unintended Consequences of "Robust" UN Peace Operations": http://communication. warpreventioninitiative.org/unintended-consequences-robust-un-peace-operations/

142. In both democracies and non-democracies, foreign military interventions reduce physical quality of life to

With that in mind, armed peacekeeping operations must be understood as a transitional step toward ultimately relying on more effective, viable nonviolent alternatives, in particular Unarmed Civilian Peacekeeping (UCP).

Rapid Reaction Force to Supplement the Blue Helmets

All peacekeeping missions must be approved by the Security Council. The UN's peacekeeping forces, the Blue Helmets, are recruited primarily from the developing nations. Several problems make them less effective than they could be. First, it takes several months to assemble a peacekeeping force, during which time the crisis can escalate dramatically. A standing, rapid reaction force that could intervene in a matter of days would solve this problem. Other problems with the Blue Helmets stem from using national forces and include a disparity of participation, armaments, tactics, command and control, and rules of engagement.

Coordinate with Civilian-Based Nonviolent Intervention Agencies

Nonviolent, civilian-based peacekeeping teams have existed for over twenty years, including the largest, the Nonviolent Peaceforce (NP), headquartered in Brussels. The NP currently has observer status at the UN and participates in discussions of peacekeeping. These organizations, including not only NP but also Peace Brigades International, Christian Peacemaker Teams and others, can sometimes go where the UN cannot and thus can be effective in particular situations. The UN needs to encourage these activities and help fund them. The UN should cooperate with other INGOs such as International Alert, Search for Common Ground, the Muslim Voice for Peace, the Jewish Voice for Peace, the Fellowship of Reconciliation, and many others by enabling their efforts to intervene early on in conflict areas. In addition to funding those efforts through UNICEF or UNHCR, much more can be done in terms of including Unarmed Civilian Peacekeeping (UCP) in mandates and recognizing and promoting the methodologies. (See section below on "Nonviolent Intervention: Utilizing Civilian Peacekeeping Forces" for a more thorough overview of the benefits of working with civilian groups.)

INTERNATIONAL LAW

"The world desperately needs a working system of governance and the closest we have to that is international law."
- Peter Weiss (International Lawyer, Peace Activist)

International Law has no defined area or governing body. It is composed of many laws, rules, and customs governing the relations between different nations, their governments, businesses, and organizations.

20% of what it was before the intervention. See: "Human Costs of Military Intervention" http://communication.warpreventioninitiative.org/human-costs-military-intervention/

It includes a piecemeal collection of customs; agreements; treaties; accords, charters such as the United Nations Charter; protocols; tribunals; memorandums; legal precedents of the International Court of Justice and more. Since there is no governing, enforcing entity, it is a largely voluntary endeavor. It includes both common law and case law. Three main principles govern international law. They are Comity (where two nations share common policy ideas, one will submit to the judicial decisions of the other); Act of State Doctrine (based on sovereignty—one State's judicial bodies will not question the policies of another State or interfere with its foreign policy); and the Doctrine of Sovereign Immunity (preventing a State's nationals from being tried in the courts of another State).

The chief problem of international law is that, being based on the anarchic principle of national sovereignty, it cannot deal very effectively with the global commons, as the failure to bring concerted action to bear on climate shift demonstrates. While it has become obvious in terms of peace and environmental dangers that we are one people forced to live together on a small, fragile planet, there is no legal entity capable of enacting statutory law, and so we must rely on negotiating ad hoc treaties to deal with problems that are systematic. Given that it is unlikely such an entity will develop in the near future, we need to strengthen the treaty regime.

Meet Study and Action Partner Peter Weiss: Promoting International Law

Peter Weiss has had a long legal career that has included significant work in constitutional and international law and human rights. He served as Vice President of the Center for Constitutional Rights, Chair of the Board of the Institute for Policy Studies, President of the American Committee on Africa, and President of the International Association of Lawyers Against Nuclear Arms. Peter argues, and his career has demonstrated, that international law may be the closest thing we have to a working system of global governance. Peter is featured in a video on Study War No More introducing a discussion exploring possibilities for effective global democratic governance, international law, and accountability. Join the discussion and check out Peter's video here: http://bit.ly/StudyWarNoMore9

Strengthen the International Court of Justice

The ICJ or "World Court" is the principal judicial body of the United Nations. It adjudicates cases submitted to it by the States and gives advisory opinions on legal matters referred to it by the UN and specialized agencies. Fifteen judges are elected for nine-year terms by the General Assembly and the Security Council. By signing the Charter, States undertake to abide by the decisions of the Court. In a submission, both State parties must agree in advance that the Court has jurisdiction, if it is to accept their submission. Decisions are only binding if both parties agree in advance to abide by them. If, after this, in the rare event that a State party does not abide by the decision, the issue may be submitted to the Security Council to determine what actions are necessary to bring the State into compliance (potentially running into a Security Council veto).

The sources of the law on which the ICJ draws for its deliberations are treaties and conventions, judicial decisions, international custom, and the teachings of international law experts. The Court can only make determinations based on existing treaty or customary law since there is no body of legislative law (there being no world legislature). This makes for tortuous decisions. When the General Assembly asked for an advisory opinion on whether the threat or use of nuclear weapons is permitted under any circumstances in international law, the Court was unable to find any treaty law that permitted or forbade the threat or use. In the end, all it could do was suggest that customary law required States to continue to negotiate on a ban. Without a body of statutory law passed by a world legislature, the Court is limited to existing treaties and customary law (which, by definition, is always behind the times) thus rendering it only mildly effective in some cases and all but useless in others.

Once again, the Security Council veto becomes a limit on the effectiveness of the Court. In the case of Nicaragua vs. The United States – the U.S. had mined Nicaragua's harbors in a clear act of war – the Court ruled against the U.S., whereupon the U.S. withdrew from compulsory jurisdiction (1986). When the matter was referred to the Security Council, the U.S. exercised its veto to avoid penalty. In effect, the five permanent members can control the outcomes of the Court should it affect them or their allies. The Court needs to be independent of the Security Council veto. When a decision needs to be enforced by the Security Council against a member, that member must recuse itself according to the ancient principle of Roman Law or Natural Justice: "No one shall be judge in his own case." [143]

The Court has also been accused of bias; the judges vote not in the pure interests of justice, but in the interests of the states that appointed them. While some of this is probably true, this criticism comes often from States that have lost their cases. Nevertheless, the more the Court follows rules of objectivity, the more weight its decisions will carry.

Cases involving aggression are usually brought not before the Court but before the Security Council, with all of its limitations. The Court needs the power to determine on its own if it has jurisdiction independent of the will of States and it then needs prosecutorial authority to bring States to the bar.

---

143. https://www.lawnotes.in/Principles_of_Natural_Justice

Strengthen the International Criminal Court

The International Criminal Court (ICC) is a permanent Court, created by a treaty, the "Rome Statute," which came into force on July 1, 2002 after ratification by 60 nations. As of 2017, the treaty has been signed by 123 nations (the "States Parties"), although not by India and China. Among the signatories, three States have declared they no longer intend to ratify the Treaty—Israel, the Republic of Sudan, and the United States. The Court is free standing and is not a part of the UN System, although it operates in partnership with it. The Security Council may refer cases to the Court, although the Court is under no obligation to investigate them. Its jurisdiction is strictly limited to crimes against humanity, war crimes, genocide, and crimes of aggression, as these have been strictly defined within the tradition of international law and as they are explicitly set out in the Statute. It is a Court of the last resort. As a general principle, the ICC may not exercise jurisdiction before a State Party has had an opportunity to try the alleged crimes itself and demonstrate capability and genuine willingness to do so, that is, the courts of the States Parties must be functional. The court is "complementary to national criminal jurisdiction" (Rome Statute, Preamble). If the Court determines that it has jurisdiction, that determination may be challenged and any investigation suspended until the challenge is heard and a determination is made. The Court may not exercise jurisdiction on the territory of any State not signatory to the Rome Statute.

The ICC is composed of four organs: the Presidency, the Office of the Prosecutor, the Registry and the Judiciary which is made up of eighteen judges in three Divisions: Pretrial, Trial, and Appeals.

The Court has come under several different criticisms. First, it has been accused of unfairly singling out atrocities in Africa while those elsewhere have been ignored. As of 2012, all seven open cases focused on African leaders. The Permanent Five of the Security Council appear to lean in the direction of this bias. As a principle, the Court must be able to demonstrate impartiality. However, two factors mitigate this criticism: 1) more African nations are party to the treaty than other nations; and 2) the Court has in fact pursued criminal allegations in Iraq and Venezuela (which did not lead to prosecutions).

A second and related criticism is that the Court appears to some to be a function of neo-colonialism as the funding and staffing are imbalanced toward the European Union and Western States. This can be addressed by spreading out the funding and the recruitment of expert staff from other nations.

Third, it has been argued that the bar for qualification of judges needs to be higher, requiring expertise in international law and prior trial experience. It is unquestionably desirable that the judges be of the highest caliber possible and have such experience. Whatever obstacles stand in the way of meeting this high standard need to be addressed.

Fourth, some argue that the powers of the Prosecutor are too broad. It should be pointed out that these were established by the Statute and would require amending to be changed. In particular, some have argued that the Prosecutor should not have a right to indict persons whose nations are not signatory; however, this appears to be a misunderstanding as the Statute limits indictment to signatories or other nations which have agreed to an indictment even if they are not signatory.

Fifth, there is no appeal to a higher court. Note that the Pre-trial chamber of the Court must agree, based on evidence, that an indictment can be made, and a defendant can appeal its findings to the Appeals Chamber. Such a case was successfully maintained by an accused in 2014 and the case dropped. However, it might be worth considering the creation of an appeals court outside of the ICC.

Sixth, there are legitimate complaints about lack of transparency. Many of the Court's sessions and proceedings are held in secret. While there may be legitimate reasons for some of this (protection of witnesses, inter alia), the highest degree of transparency possible is required and the Court needs to review its procedures in this regard.

Seventh, some critics have argued that the standards of due process are not up to the highest standards of practice. If this is the case, it must be corrected.

Eighth, others have argued that the Court has achieved too little for the amount of money it has spent, having obtained only one conviction to date. This, however, is an argument for the Court's respect for process and its inherently conservative nature. It has clearly not gone on witch-hunts for every nasty person in the world but has shown admirable restraint. It is also a testimony to the difficulty of bringing these prosecutions and assembling evidence, sometimes years after the fact of massacres and other atrocities, especially in a multicultural setting.

Finally, the heaviest criticism laid against the Court is its very existence as a transnational institution; an implied limitation on unconfined State sovereignty. But so, too, is every treaty, and they are all, including the Rome Statute, entered into voluntarily and for the common good. Ending war cannot be achieved by sovereign states alone. The record of millennia shows nothing but failure in that regard. Transnational judicial institutions are a necessary part of an Alternative Global Security System. Of course, the Court must be subject to the same norms which they would advocate for the rest of the global community, that is, transparency, accountability, speedy and due process, and highly qualified personnel.

The establishment of the International Criminal Court was a major step forward in the construction of a functioning peace system.

It needs to be emphasized that the ICC remains a very new institution, the first iteration of an international community's efforts to assure that the world's most egregious criminals do not get away with their mass crimes. Even the United Nations, which is the second iteration of collective security, is still evolving and still in need of serious reform.

Civil society organizations are at the forefront of reform efforts. The Coalition for the International Criminal Court consists of 2,500 civil society organizations in 150 countries advocating for a fair, effective, and independent ICC and improved access to justice for victims of genocide, war crimes and crimes against humanity. The American Non-Governmental Organizations Coalition for the International Criminal Court is a coalition of non-governmental organizations committed to advocating for full United States support for the International Criminal Court and the earliest possible U.S. ratification of the Court's Rome Statute.[144]

Encourage Compliance with Existing Treaties

Crucial treaties for controlling war that are now in force are not recognized by a few critical nations. In particular, the Convention on the Prohibition of the Use, Stockpiling, Production and Transfer of Anti-Personnel Mines and on their Destruction is not recognized by the United States, Russia and China. The Rome Statute of the International Criminal Court is not recognized by the United States, Sudan, and Israel. Russia has not ratified it. India and China are holdouts, as are a number of other members of the UN. While holdout States argue that the court might be biased against them, the only plausible reason for a nation not becoming a party to the Statute is that it reserves the right to commit war crimes, genocide, crimes against humanity or aggression, or to define such acts as not coming under the common definitions of such acts. These States must be pressured by global citizens to come to the table and play by the same rules as the rest of humanity. States must also be pressured to comply with human rights law and with the various Geneva Conventions. The non-complying states, including the U.S., need to ratify the Comprehensive Test Ban Treaty and reassert the validity of the existing Kellogg-Briand Pact that already outlaws war.

The importance of demanding compliance with existing treaties is demonstrated by the brazen lack of compliance by the U.S. regarding the Optional Protocol to the Convention on the Rights of the Child on the Involvement of Children in Armed Conflict, (OPAC).[145]

Article 3.3 of the treaty requires military recruitment of minors to be carried out with the informed consent of the child's parents or legal guardians. Meanwhile, American high school youth are often required to take the military's entrance exam during school hours without parental knowledge or consent. Mandatory military testing without mom and dad's O.K. is

---

144. http://www.iccnow.org/; http://www.amicc.org/

145. Optional Protocol to the Convention on the Rights of the Child on the involvement of children in armed

a violation of the Convention. Despite robust propaganda stating otherwise, the American military struggles to fill its ranks so it feels compelled to resort to deceptive recruiting measures. Data gained from the Pentagon through a Freedom of Information Act request identifies a thousand American high schools that require students to take the military's enlistment exam. It is strongly encouraged in 11,000 others.

The UN's Committee on the Rights of the Child called on the U.S. to ensure the voluntary nature of military testing in the high schools in remarks adopted by the Committee at its sixty-second session (January 2013) regarding the Optional Protocol on the Involvement of Children in Armed Conflict.

The committee also expressed alarm that American high school children are being involuntarily placed into the Junior Reserve Officers Training Corps (JROTC) program. The committee calls on the U.S. to ensure that families and children are properly informed of the voluntary nature of the JROTC program. In its response to the committee, the U.S. denied the existence of forced military testing in the schools and it denied the involuntary placement of children into the JROTC program.[146]

Create New Treaties

The evolving situation will always require the consideration of new treaties, the legal relations between the different parties. Two that should be taken up immediately are:

1.   Control Greenhouse Gases

New treaties are necessary to deal with global climate shift and its consequences, in particular a treaty governing the emission of all greenhouse gases that includes assistance for the developing nations.

2.   Pave the Way for Climate Refugees

A related but separate treaty will need to deal with the rights of climate refugees to migrate both internally and internationally. This applies to the urgency of the ongoing effects of climate change, but also the current refugee crises emerging from the Middle East and North Africa, where historical and current Western policies contributed immensely to war and violence. As long as war exists, there will be refugees. The United Nations Convention on Refugees legally obligates signatories to take in refugees. This provision requires compliance but given the overwhelming numbers that will be involved, it needs to include provisions for assistance if major conflicts are to be avoided. This assistance could be part of a Global Development Plan as described below.

conflict: http://www.ohchr.org/EN/ProfessionalInterest/Pages/OPACCRC.aspx

146. See more at National Coalition to Protect Student Privacy at http://www.studentprivacy.org/child-soldier-protocol.html

Establish Truth and Reconciliation Commissions

When interstate or civil war occurs in spite of the many barriers the Alternative Global Security System throws up, the various mechanisms outlined above will work quickly to bring an end to overt hostilities, restoring order. Following that, paths to reconciliation are necessary to ensure that there is no relapse into direct and indirect violence. The following processes are considered necessary for reconciliation:

- Uncovering the truth of what happened

- Acknowledgement by the offender(s) of harm done

- Remorse expressed in apology to victim(s)

- Forgiveness

- Justice in some form

- Planning to prevent recurrence

- Resuming constructive aspects of the relationship

- Rebuilding trust over time[147]

Truth and Reconciliation Commissions are a form of transitional justice that offer an alternative path to prosecutions, and counteract cultures of denial.[148] They have been set

147. Santa-Barbara, J. (2007). Reconciliation. In: *Handbook of peace and conflict studies*, edited by Charles Webel and Johan Galtung, 173–86. New York: Routledge.

148. Fischer, M. (2015). Transitional Justice and Reconciliation: Theory and Practice. In *The contemporary conflict resolution reader*, edited by Miall, H., Woodhouse, T., Ramsbotham, O., and Mitchell, C. Cambridge: Polity. (325–33).

up in more than 20 countries. Such commissions have already worked in many situations in Ecuador, Canada, the Czech Republic, and most notably in South Africa at the end of the Apartheid regime.[149] Such commissions take the place of criminal proceedings and act to begin to restore trust so that genuine peace, rather than a simple cessation of hostilities, can actually commence. Their function is to establish the facts of past wrongdoing by all actors, both the injured and the perpetrators (who may confess in return for clemency) in order to prevent any historical revisionism and to remove any causes for a new outbreak of violence motivated by revenge. The public and official exposure of truth contributes to social and personal healing; engages all of society in national dialog; examines the ills of society that made abuses possible; and provides a sense of public ownership in the process.[150]

THE ROLE OF GLOBAL CIVIL SOCIETY AND INTERNATIONAL NGOS

Civil society usually encompasses actors in professional associations, clubs, unions, faith-based organizations, non-governmental organizations (NGOs), clans, and other community groups.[151] Those are mostly found on a local/national level, and together with global civil society networks and campaigns, they form an unprecedented infrastructure to challenge war and militarism.

In 1900, there were a handful of global civil institutions, such as the International Postal Union and the Red Cross. Since then, there has been an astonishing rise of international non-governmental organizations devoted to peacebuilding and peacekeeping. There are now thousands of these INGOs including such organizations as: the Nonviolent Peaceforce, Greenpeace, Servicio Paz y Justicia, Peace Brigades International, the Women's International League for Peace and Freedom, Global Network of Women Peacebuilders, Veterans For Peace, the Fellowship of Reconciliation, the Hague Appeal for Peace, Global Campaign for Peace Education, the International Peace Bureau, Muslim Peacemaker Teams, Jewish Voice for Peace, Oxfam International, Doctors Without Borders, Pace e Bene, Ploughshares Fund, Apopo, Citizens for Global Solutions, International Institute on Peace Education, Nukewatch, the Carter Center, the Conflict Resolution Center International, the Natural Step, Transition Towns, United Nations Association, Rotary International, Women's Action for New Directions, Peace Direct, the American Friends Service Committee, and countless other smaller and

149. Reconciliation through Restorative Justice: Analyzing South Africa's Truth and Reconciliation Process -http://www.beyondintractability.org/library/reconciliation-through-restorative-justice-analyzing-south-africas-truth-and-reconciliation

150. Fischer, M. (2015). Transitional Justice and Reconciliation: Theory and Practice. In The contemporary conflict resolution reader, edited by Miall, H., Woodhouse, T., Ramsbotham, O., and Mitchell, C. Cambridge: Polity. (325–33)

151. See Paffenholz, T. (2010). Civil society & peacebuilding: a critical assessment. Boulder, CO: Lynne Ryner. The case studies in this book examine the role of civil society peacebuilding efforts in conflict zones such as Northern Ireland, Cyprus, Israel and Palestine, Afghanistan, Sri Lanka, and Somalia.

less well known ones including the Blue Mountain Project or the War Prevention Initiative. The Nobel Peace Committee recognized the importance of global civil society organizations, awarding several of them with the Nobel Peace Prize.

A heartening example is the founding of Combatants for Peace:

> *The "Combatants for Peace" movement was started jointly by Palestinians and Israelis, who have taken an active part in the cycle of violence; Israelis as soldiers in the Israeli army (IDF) and Palestinians as part of the violent struggle for Palestinian freedom. After brandishing weapons for so many years, and having seen one another only through weapon sights, we have decided to put down our guns, and to fight for peace.*

We can also look at how individuals like Jody Williams harnessed the power of global citizen-diplomacy to help the international community agree on the global ban on land-mines, or how a delegation of citizen-diplomats is building people-to-people bridges between Russians and Americans amidst heightened international tensions in 2016.[152]

These individuals and organizations knit the world together into a pattern of care and concern, opposing war and injustice, and working for peace, justice and a sustainable economy.[153] These organizations are not only advocates for peace; they work on the ground to successfully mediate, resolve, or transform conflicts and build peace. They are recognized as a global force for good. Many are accredited to the United Nations. Aided by the World Wide Web, they are the proof of an emerging consciousness of planetary citizenship.

Nonviolent Intervention: Utilizing Civilian Peacekeeping Forces

For over 20 years, trained, nonviolent and unarmed civilian forces have been invited to intervene in conflicts around the world to provide protection for human rights defenders and peace workers by maintaining a high-profile physical presence accompanying threatened individuals and organizations. Since these organizations are not associated with any government, and since their personnel are drawn from many countries and have no agenda other than creating a safe space where dialogue can occur between conflicting parties, they have a credibility that national governments lack.

---

152. The Center for Citizen Initiatives began a series of citizen-to-citizen initiatives and exchanges, buttressed by official media PR and social media networks across the United States and Russia. See also: Tennison, S. (2012). *The power of impossible ideas: Ordinary citizens' extraordinary efforts to avert international crisis.* Odenwald Press.

153. For more, see the book on the development of the huge, unnamed movement *Blessed Unrest* (2007) by Paul Hawken.

Meet Study and Action Partner Tiffany Easthom: Executive Director, Nonviolent Peaceforce

Prior to her current role as Executive Director, Tiffany served as Program Director for Nonviolent Peaceforce's Middle East program, and Country Director in South Sudan and Sri Lanka. Tiffany holds a BA in Justice Studies and a MA Degree in Human Security and Peacebuilding from Royal Roads University in Victoria, British Columbia, Canada. She also studied peacebuilding in the field in Uganda and served as Country Director for Peace Brigades International in Indonesia. Nonviolent Peaceforce's unarmed civilian peacekeeping approach provides an effective, more sustainable, and potentially transformative alternative to militarized peacekeeping. Tiffany is featured in a video on Study War No More introducing a discussion exploring the viability of civilian-based defense and unarmed civilian peacekeeping as alternatives to war and military-based defense. Join the discussion and check out Tiffany's video here: http://bit.ly/StudyWarNoMore11

By being nonviolent and unarmed, they present no physical threat to others and can go where armed peacekeepers might provoke a violent clash. They provide an open space, dialogue with government authorities and armed forces, and create a link between local peace workers and the international community. Initiated in 1981, Peace Brigades International has current projects in Guatemala, Honduras, New Mexico, Nepal and Kenya.

The Nonviolent Peaceforce was founded in 2000 and is headquartered in Brussels. NP has four goals for its work: to create a space for lasting peace, to protect civilians, to develop and promote the theory and practice of unarmed civilian peacekeeping so that it may be adopted as a policy option by decision makers and public institutions, and to build the pool of professionals able to join peace teams through regional activities, training, and maintaining a roster of trained, available people. NP currently has teams in the Philippines, Myanmar, South Sudan, and Syria.

For example, the Nonviolent Peaceforce currently operates its largest project in civil-war South Sudan. Unarmed civilian protectors successfully accompany women collecting firewood in conflict zones, where fighting parties use rape as a weapon of war. Three or four unarmed civilian protectors have proven to be 100% successful in preventing those forms of wartime rape. Mel Duncan, co-founder of the Nonviolent Peaceforce, recounts another example of South Sudan:

"[Derek and Andreas] were with 14 women and children, when the area where they were with these people was attacked by a militia. They took the 14 women and children in a tent, while people outside were shot point blank. On three occasions, rebel militia came to Andreas and Derek and pointed AK47s at their heads and said, 'you have to go, we want those people'. And on all three occasions, very calmly, Andreas and Derek held up their Nonviolent Peaceforce identity badges and said: "we are unarmed, we are here to protect civilians, and we will not leave'. After the third time the militia left, and the people were spared."

Such stories bring up the question of risk to unarmed civilian peacekeepers. One certainly cannot create a more threatening scenario than the previous one. Yet Nonviolent Peaceforce has had five conflict-related injuries - three of which were accidental - in thirteen years of operating. Moreover, it is safe to assume that an armed protection in the example described would have resulted in the deaths of Derek and Andreas as well as those they sought to protect.

Photo: Nonviolent Peaceforce

These and other organizations, such as Christian Peacemaker Teams, provide a model that can be scaled up to take the place of armed peacekeepers and other forms of violent intervention. They are a perfect example of the role that civil society is already playing in keeping the peace. Beyond providing physical protection and participating in dialogue processes, these groups contribute to the very reconstruction of the social fabric in conflict zones.

To date, these crucial efforts are under-recognized and underfunded. They need to be fully sanctioned by the UN and other institutions and by international law. These are among the most promising efforts to protect civilians, create space for civil society, and contribute to lasting peace.

Create a Nonviolent, Civilian-Based Defense Force

Nonviolence scholar Gene Sharp combed history to find and record hundreds of methods that have been used successfully to thwart oppression. His search led him to the vision of Civilian-Based Defense (CBD); an alternative system that could serve the "security" functions supposedly provided by the War System. CBD:

> "...indicates defense by civilians (as distinct from military personnel) using civilian means of struggle (as distinct from military and paramilitary means). This is a policy intended to deter and defeat foreign military invasions, occupations, and internal usurpations."[154] This defense "is meant to be waged by the population and its institutions on the basis of advance preparation, planning, and training."

> It is a "policy [in which] the whole population and the society's institutions become the fighting forces. Their weaponry consists of a vast variety of forms of psychological, economic, social, and political resistance and counter-attack. This policy aims to deter attacks and to defend against them by preparations to make the society unrulable by would-be tyrants and aggressors. The trained population and the society's institutions would be prepared to deny the attackers their objectives and to make consolidation of political control impossible. These aims would be achieved by applying massive and selective noncooperation and defiance.

> In addition, where possible, the defending country would aim to create maximum international problems for the attackers and to subvert the reliability of their troops and functionaries" (Gene Sharp, Author, Founder of Albert Einstein Institution).

The dilemma faced by all societies since the invention of war, namely, to either submit or become a mirror image of the attacking aggressor, is solved by CBD. Becoming as or more war-like than the aggressor is based on the fact that stopping the aggressor requires coercion. CBD deploys a powerful coercive force that does not require military action.

In CBD, all cooperation is withdrawn from the invading power. Nothing works. The lights don't come on, or the heat, the waste is not picked up, the transit system doesn't work, courts cease to function, the people don't obey orders. This is what happened in the "Kapp Putsch" in Berlin in 1920 when a would-be dictator and his private army tried to take over. The previous government fled, but the citizens of Berlin made governing so impossible that, even with overwhelming military power, the takeover collapsed in weeks. All power does not come from the barrel of a gun.

In some cases, sabotage against government property would be deemed appropriate. When the French Army occupied Germany in the aftermath of World War I, German railway workers disabled engines and tore up tracks to prevent the French from moving troops around to confront large-scale demonstrations. If a French soldier got on a tram, the driver refused to move.

---

154. Sharp, G. (1990). *Civilian-Based Defense: A post-military weapons system.* Link to entire book: http:// www. aeinstein.org/wp-content/uploads/2013/09/Civilian-Based-Defense-English.pdf.

Two core realities support CBD; first, that all power comes from below—all government is by consent of the governed and that consent can always be withdrawn, causing the collapse of a governing elite. Second, if a nation is seen as ungovernable, because of a robust CBD force, there is no reason to try to conquer it. A nation defended by military power can be defeated in war by a superior military power. Countless examples exist. Examples also exist of peoples rising up and defeating ruthless dictatorial governments through nonviolent struggle, beginning with the liberation from an occupying power in India by Gandhi's people power movement, continuing with the overthrow of the Marcos regime in the Philippines, the Soviet-backed dictatorships in Eastern Europe, and the Arab Spring, to name only a few of the most notable examples.

In a CBD all able adults are trained in methods of resistance.[155] A standing Reserve Corps of millions is organized, making the nation so strong in its independence that no one would think of trying to conquer it. A CBD system is widely publicized and totally transparent to adversaries. A CBD system would cost a fraction of the amount now spent to fund a military defense system. CBD can provide effective defense within the War System, while it is an essential component of a robust peace system. Certainly one can argue that nonviolent defense must transcend the nation-state focus as a form of social defense, since the nation state itself often is an instrument of oppression against physical or cultural existence of peoples.[156]

As noted previously, scientifically proven wisdom holds that nonviolent civil resistance is twice as likely to be successful compared to movements that use violence. The contemporary knowledge, in theory and practice, is what makes longtime nonviolent movement activist and scholar George Lakey hopeful for a strong role of CBD. He states: "If the peace movements of Japan, Israel and the United States choose to build on a half century of strategy work and devise a serious alternative to war, they will certainly build in preparation and training and gain the attention of pragmatists in their societies."[157]

PROPOSALS FOR STARTING OVER: ALTERNATIVE APPROACHES TO HUMANE GLOBAL GOVERNANCE

Establishing a new security paradigm requires critique and consideration of what exists and what might be. We've given significant attention to reforming the United Nations, our present and most hopeful form of global governance. However, we must also take into consideration the failures of the UN, many of which stem from inherent problems with

---

155. See Gene Sharp, The Politics of Nonviolent Action, and Making Europe Unconquerable, and Civilian Based Defense among other works. One booklet, From Dictatorship to Democracy was translated into Arabic prior to the Arab Spring

156. See Burrowes, Robert J. 1996. The Strategy of Nonviolent Defense: A Gandhian Approach for a comprehensive approach to nonviolent defense. The author considers CBD strategically flawed.

157. See George Lakey: Does Japan really need to expand its military to solve its security dilemma? http://

collective security as a model for keeping or restoring the peace. This foundation may be too much to overcome, so we must also consider new, alternative forms of global governance to serve the critical function of creating and keeping the peace.

Inherent Problems with Collective Security

The United Nations is based on the principle of collective security, that is, when a nation threatens or initiates aggression, the other nations will bring to bear preponderant force acting as a deterrent, or as a very early remedy for an invasion by defeating the aggressor on the battlefield. This is, of course, a militarized solution, threatening or carrying out a larger war to deter or prevent a smaller war. The one principal example– the Korean War – was a failure. The war dragged on for years and the border remains heavily militarized. In fact, the war has never been formally terminated. Collective security is simply a tweaking of the existing system of using violence to attempt to counter violence. It actually requires a militarized world so that the world body has armies it can call on. Moreover, while the UN is theoretically based on this system, it is not designed to execute it, since it has no duty to do so in the event of conflicts. It has only an opportunity to act and that is severely enervated by the Security Council veto. Five privileged member states can, and very often have, exercised their own national aims, rather than agreed to cooperate for the common good. This partially explains why the UN has failed to stop so many wars since its founding. This, along with its other weaknesses, explains why some people think humanity needs to start over with a far more democratic institution that has the power to enact and enforce statutory law and bring about peaceful resolution of conflicts.

Principles of Humane Global Governance

"The contemporary quest for humane governance builds on kindred efforts in the past, while rooted in an unfolding present, and above all aspiring to achieve an imagined future. The idea of humane governance is itself a way of expressing this process that is sensitive to the shortcomings, achievements, and gropings toward human betterment on this planet."
-Richard Falk, Professor of International Law

Richard Falk, an early contributor to the World Orders Model Project (affectionately known as WOMP), argued that the pursuit of humane global governance was a "normative project," one that "posits an imagined community for the whole of humanity which overcomes the most problematic aspects of the present world scene."[158] WOMP sought to consider and design new models of world order rooted in four fundamental values: 1) peace, 2) economic

---

wagingnonviolence.org/feature/japan-military-expand-civilian-based-defense/

158. See: Falk, R. (1995). *On Humane Governance: Toward a New Global Politics*. University Park, PA: Penn State University Press.

well-being, 3) social and political justice, and 4) environmental sustainability. These world order values identify the purposes and functions of global governance and serve as the criteria from which to assess alternative approaches. Falk suggested that this normative project has 10 dimensions – many of which we have taken up in our outline of a global security system.

10 Dimensions of the "Normative Project" of Humane Governance

1. Taming war

2. Abolishing war

3. Making individuals accountable

4. Collective Security

5. Rule of Law

6. Nonviolent revolutionary politics

7. Human Rights

8. Stewardship of nature

9. Positive Citizenship

10. Cosmopolitan democracy

World BEYOND War and other networks have developed visions and frameworks for global governance that address many of these dimensions. The Earth Federation and World BEYOND War's draft proposal for a Global Emergency Assembly are introduced below.

The Earth Federation & The Earth Constitution

The World Constitution and Parliament Association (WCPA), founded in 1958, drafted The Constitution for the Federation of Earth[159] that was ratified in 1977 at the World Constituent Assembly and amended in 1991. WCPA has since been advocating for its ratification around the world.

> *"The principle of unity in diversity is the basis for a new age when war shall be outlawed and peace prevail; when the earth's total resources shall be equitably used for human welfare; and when basic human rights and responsibilities shall be shared by all without discrimination."*
> *- The Preamble to the Earth Constitution*

---

159. Read the Constitution for the Federation of Earth ("The Earth Constitution") in its entirety here: http://earth-constitution.org/constitution/english/

A Global Security System: An Alternative to War 2018-19 Edition

Article 1 of The Earth Constitution outlines the broad functions of the Federation of Earth:

1. To prevent war, secure disarmament, and resolve territorial and other disputes which endanger peace and human rights.

2. To protect universal human rights, including life, liberty, security, democracy, and equal opportunities in life.

3. To obtain for all people on earth the conditions required for equitable economic and social development and for diminishing social differences.

4. To regulate world trade, communications, transportation, currency, standards, use of world resources, and other global and international processes.

5. To protect the environment and the ecological fabric of life from all sources of damage, and to control technological innovations whose effects transcend national boundaries, for the purpose of keeping Earth a safe, healthy and happy home for humanity.

6. To devise and implement solutions to all problems which are beyond the capacity of national governments, or which are now or may become of global or international concern or consequence.

The World Parliament

House of Peoples	House of Counselors	House of Nations
1000 delegates by population	Delegates from around the world: 200	1, 2 or 3 Delegates from each nation

World Judiciary   World Executive   World Police   World Ombudsmus

The Integrative Complex

The World Administration

Outline of the structure for an Earth Federation government established by The Earth Constitution.

Article 2 describes the basic structure, positing that The Federation of Earth shall be universal of all nations and peoples; be non-military and democratic in structure; with authority limited to "problems and affairs which transcend national boundaries, leaving to national governments jurisdiction over the internal affairs of the respective nations but consistent with the authority of the World Government to protect universal human rights as defined in this World Constitution." The Constitution is rich in detail, describing specific organs, powers and means of enforcement. A World Parliament, functioning as a legislative body, is comprised of three houses:

1. A House of Peoples (with 1000 electoral districts representing all people everywhere).

2. A House of Nations (preserving the identity and integrity of each nation).

3. A House of Counselors (200 representatives from around the world representing the whole of the planet).

The parliament is supported by 4 main agencies:

1. The World Executive (run by 5 elected persons, one from each Continent) with no military power and no power to suspend the Constitution. The World Executive (with the help of World Civil Service) runs the Integrative Complex (dedicated to coordinating all agencies of government) and the World Administration (departments necessary to deal with all world affairs as determined by the World Parliament).

2. The World Judiciary (a World Supreme Court system with universal jurisdiction and 8 specialized benches).

3. The Enforcement System with World Police and Attorneys General (run by five heads drawn from each continental division) who enforce world law using only weapons necessary to apprehend individuals.

4. The World Ombudsmus is run by five heads drawn from each continental division (an entire worldwide agency dedicated to protecting and promoting human rights everywhere on Earth).

Proposal for a Global Emergency Assembly

Another framework for global governance is World BEYOND War's vision for a Global Emergency Assembly (GEA)[160]. Although a work in progress, we share a short summary of it here, along with the proposals above, in hopes of stimulating much needed alternative thinking on approaches to global governance.

GEA is intended to replace the United Nations and related institutions. The design of GEA balances representation of nations with representation of people, also engaging with local and provincial governments that tend to be more representative than national ones. The Global Emergency Assembly does not, in its structure, favor any existing government over any

---

160. The Global Emergency Assembly was submitted as an entry to the Global Challenges Prize managed by the Global Challenges Foundation. World BEYOND War is working to hone this vision. Copies of the full, more detailed proposal are available upon request.

A Global Security System: An Alternative to War 2018-19 Edition

other, or create laws that impact other governments, businesses, or individuals beyond what is *necessary to prevent global catastrophe*.

GEA consists of two representative bodies, an educational-scientific-cultural organization, and several smaller committees. The People's Assembly (PA) consists of 5,000 members, each of whom represents the population of a coherent geographic area with a near-equivalent population of voters. PA members are elected with maximum participation, fairness, transparency, choice, and verifiability. The Nations' Assembly (NA) consists of approximately 200 members, each of whom represents a national government. Members serve two-year terms with elections or appointments in even-numbered years. NA members are elected or appointed by national publics, government bodies, or rulers as each nation determines.

A democratic global institution without a military or the power to mobilize militaries should not threaten national interests but rather allow nations the means to circumvent their own weaknesses. Governments that choose not to join will be left out of global decision making. National governments will not be permitted to join the NA unless their people and regional and local governments have complete freedom to participate in and fund the PA.

The GEA Educational Scientific and Cultural Organization (GEAESCO) is overseen by a five-member board serving staggered 10-year terms and elected by the two assemblies -- which also retain the power to remove and replace GEAESCO board members.

Members of both assemblies and of GEAESCO are required to obtain training in nonviolent communication, conflict resolution, and dialogue/deliberation methods for the common good.

The assemblies identify global / common issues and problems to be addressed. Examples might be war, environmental destruction, starvation, disease, population growth, and mass homelessness. GEAESCO makes recommendations for each project, and also identifies areas of the world that are having the most success in working on each project. Assembly members from those areas of the world will have the first option of joining the relevant committees. Committees of 45, including 30 PA members and 15 NA members, pursue GEA's work on particular projects. GEAESCO is also tasked with organizing an annual competition for development of the best educational, scientific, or cultural creations in the area of each project.

GEA maintains five meeting locations around the world, rotating assembly meetings among them, and allowing committees to meet in multiple locations connected by video and audio. Both assemblies make decisions by public, recorded, majority vote, and together they have the power to create (or dissolve) committees and to delegate work to those committees.

GEA's resources come from payments made by local and regional, but not national, governments. These payments are required in order for the residents of any jurisdiction to participate, and are determined on the basis of ability to pay.

GEA seeks compliance with global laws and participation in global projects on the part of governments at every level, as well as businesses, and individuals. In doing so, it is bound by its constitution to forego the use of violence, the threat of violence, the sanctioning of violence, or any complicity in preparations for the use of violence. The same constitution requires respecting the rights of future generations, of children, and of the natural environment.

Tools for creating compliance include moral pressure, praise, and condemnation; positions on committees for those areas of the world performing the best on the relevant work; rewards in the form of investments; punishment in the form of leading and organizing divestments and boycotts; the practice of restorative justice in arbitration hearings and prosecutions; the creation of truth-and-reconciliation commissions; and the ultimate sanction of banishment from representation in GEA. Many of these tools are implemented by a GEA Court, whose panels of judges are elected by the GEA assemblies.

WORLDBEYONDWAR.org
a global movement to end all wars

CREATING A CULTURE OF PEACE

EXECUTIVE SUMMARY

Article 2 of the UN Declaration and Programme of Action on a Culture of Peace observes that "progress in the fuller development of a culture of peace comes about through values, attitudes, modes of behaviour and ways of life conducive to the promotion of peace among individuals, groups and nations." These are the essential elements pursued by this component of our system. A culture of peace also helps us to establish the vision and guiding principles of the world we prefer and desire. In our engaged activism it is easy to direct our energy almost entirely toward resistance to that which we oppose; this is done at the expense of reflecting on and designing the alternatives. Frameworks previously explored, including common security, human security, ecological security and nonviolence comprise the ethical and normative criteria for assessing the alternative approaches and strategies described throughout this book. In this section we begin to identify and tell the "new story" and peaceful evolutions that have been emerging. These positive trends give us hope and inspiration that peaceful change is indeed possible. Educational efforts supporting planetary citizenship establish a foundation of interconnection and interdependence on our shared planet. Formal and non-formal peace education and peace research are primary tools for writing the "software" of our peace system. In this section we also introduce and advocate for responsible peace journalism; a proactive approach to news reporting that emphasizes illuminating the underlying causes of conflict, frames conflicts in terms of their complexity, and seeks to publicize peace initiatives commonly ignored by the mainstream press. Finally, we examine the role and potential of religion as a tool for peacebuilding – rather than a cause of violence.

STRATEGIC POLICY AND ACTION RECOMMENDATIONS

• Encourage adoption of local, state, and national plans of action supporting the achievement of the principles of the UN Declaration and Programme of Action on a Culture of Peace.

• Support the development of curricula encouraging understanding of planetary citizenship.

• Provide increased funding for peace research.

• Advocate for the universalization of peace education into all formal and non-formal settings and teacher training institutions.

• Support responsible media outlets that promote peace journalism.

• Get the word out on "The New Story" that is emerging.

•Encourage religiously motivated peacemaking and peacebuilding.

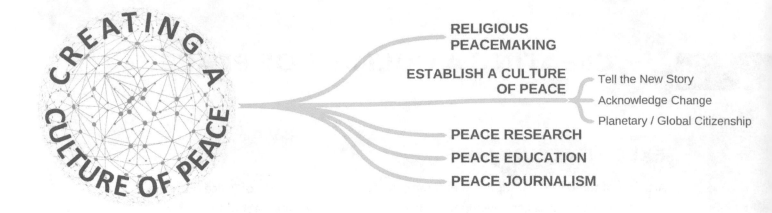

RELIGIOUS PEACEMAKING

ESTABLISH A CULTURE OF PEACE
— Tell the New Story
— Acknowledge Change
— Planetary / Global Citizenship

PEACE RESEARCH

PEACE EDUCATION

PEACE JOURNALISM

Many of the approaches outlined here address what Thomas Merton called the "climate of thought": the current values and frameworks that normalize violence in society.

ESTABLISHING A CULTURE OF PEACE

"Put in the simplest possible terms, a peace culture is a culture that promotes peaceable diversity. Such a culture includes lifeways, patterns of belief, values, behavior, and accompanying institutional arrangements that promote mutual caring and well-being as well as an equality that includes appreciation of difference, stewardship, and equitable sharing of the resources... It offers mutual security for humankind in all its diversity through a profound sense of species identity as well as kinship with the living earth. There is no need for violence."
- Elise Boulding (Founding figure of Peace and Conflict Studies)

A culture of peace is contrasted with a warrior culture, also known as a dominator society, where warrior gods instruct the people to create hierarchies of rank so that men dominate other men, men dominate women, there is constant competition and frequent physical violence, and nature is seen as something to be conquered. In a warrior culture, safety is only for those individuals or nations that are at the top, if they can stay there. No society is completely one or the other, but in today's world the tilt is toward the warrior societies, making necessary the growth of a culture of peace if humanity is to survive. Societies that socialize their children for aggressive behavior make wars more likely, and in a vicious circle, wars socialize people for aggression.

"Every relationship of domination, of exploitation, of oppression is by
definition violent, whether or not the violence is expressed by drastic means.
In such a relationship, dominator and dominated alike are reduced to things
– the former dehumanized by an excess of power, the latter by a lack of it.
And things cannot love."
- Paulo Freire (Brazilian Popular Educator)

In 1999, the United Nations General Assembly approved a Programme of Action on a Culture of Peace.[161] Article I further defines it:

A culture of peace is a set of values, attitudes, traditions and modes of behavior and ways of life based on:

1. Respect for life, ending of violence and promotion and practice of nonviolence through education, dialogue and cooperation.

2. Full respect for the principles of sovereignty, territorial integrity and political independence of States and non-intervention in matters which are essentially within the domestic jurisdiction of any State, in accordance with the Charter of the United Nations and international law.

3. Full respect for and promotion of all human rights and fundamental freedoms.

4. Commitment to peaceful settlement of conflicts.

5. Efforts to meet the developmental and environmental needs of present and future generations.

6. Respect for and promotion of the right to development.

7. Respect for and promotion of equal rights and opportunities for women and men.

8. Respect for and promotion of the right of everyone to freedom of expression, opinion and information.

9. Adherence to the principles of freedom, justice, democracy, tolerance, solidarity, cooperation, pluralism, cultural diversity, dialogue and understanding at all levels of society and among nations; fostered by an enabling.

The General Assembly identified eight action areas:

1. Fostering a culture of peace through education.

2. Promoting sustainable economic and social development.

3. Promoting respect for all human rights.

4. Ensuring equality between women and men.

---

161. The valuable ideals of the United Nations and its Culture of Peace initiative need to be acknowledged, despite the UN's organizational imperfection outlined earlier.

5. Fostering democratic participation.

6. Advancing understanding, tolerance and solidarity.

7. Supporting participatory communication and the free flow of information and knowledge.

8. Promoting international peace and security.

The Global Movement for the Culture of Peace is a partnership of groups from civil society that have banded together to promote a culture of peace. Part of the work is to tell a new story.

Meet Study and Action Partner Ambassador Anwarul Chowdury: Nurturing a Global Culture of Peace

Ambassador Anwarul K. Chowdhury is an inspirational champion for sustainable peace and development and has ardently advanced the cause of the Global Movement for the Culture of Peace that has energized civil society all over the world. He served as Ambassador and Permanent Representative of Bangladesh to the United Nations in New York from 1996 to 2001 and as the Under-Secretary-General and High Representative of the United Nations, responsible for the most vulnerable countries of the world from 2002 to 2007. He led the effort for adoption within the United Nations General Assembly of the landmark Declaration and Programme of Action on a Culture of Peace (1999), and in 1998 for the proclamation of the "International Decade for a Culture of Peace and Nonviolence for the Children of the World (2001-2010)." Ambassador Chowdhury is featured in a video on Study War No More introducing a discussion on how alternative visions, including the culture of peace and human security, can aid in shaping an alternative global security system. Join the discussion and check out Ambassador Chowdhury's video here: http://bit.ly/StudyWarNoMore4

Telling a New Story

"The deepest crises experienced by any society are those moments of change when the story becomes inadequate for meeting the survival demands of a present situation."
- Thomas Berry ("Earth Scholar")

Crucial to further developing a culture of peace is the telling of a new story about humanity and the earth. The old story, beloved by governments and too many journalists and teachers, is that the world is a dangerous place, that war has always been with us, is inevitable, in our genes, and good for the economy, that preparing for war ensures peace, that it's impossible to end war, that the global economy is a dog-eat-dog competition and if you don't win you lose, that resources are scarce and if you want to live well you must grab them, often by force, and that nature is simply a mine of raw materials. This story is a fatalistic self-fulfilling deterministic outlook that claims to be realism but is in fact defeatist pessimism.

In the old story, history is presented as little more than a succession of wars. As peace educator Darren Reiley puts it:

> "The assumption that war is a natural and necessary force of human progress is deeply ingrained and continues to be reinforced by the way we teach history. In the U.S., the content standards for teaching American History go like this: 'Cause and consequences of the American Revolutionary War, the War of 1812, the Civil War, World War I, the Great Depression (and how World War II ended it), Civil Rights, war, war, war.' Taught this way, war becomes the unquestioned driver of social change, but it is an assumption that needs to be challenged, or students will take it for the truth."

All the cooperative endeavors of humanity, the long periods of peace, the existence of peaceful societies, the development of conflict resolution skills, and the remarkable stories of successful nonviolence are all ignored in the traditional recounting of the past that can only be described as "warist." Fortunately, historians from the Council on Peace Research in History and others have begun revising this view, bringing to light the reality of peace in our history.

There is a new story, backed up by science and experience. In fact, war is a relatively recent social invention. We humans have been around for over 100,000 years but there is little evidence for warfare, and certainly interstate warfare, going back much more than 6,000 years, very few known earlier instances of warlike activities dating back 10,000 years, and none earlier.[162] For 95 percent of our history we were without war, indicating that war is not genetic, but cultural. Even during the worst period of wars we have seen, the 20th century,

---

162. There is not one single authoritative source providing evidence for the birth of warfare. Numerous archeological and anthropological studies provide ranges from 12,000 to 6,000 year or less. We adhere to the generalized conclusion that there is scant and rapidly disappearing archaeological evidence of lethal group violence prior to 10,000 years ago. It would go beyond the scope of this book to enter the debate. A good overview of selected sources is provided by: Horgan, J. (2012). *The end of war.* San Francisco, CA: McSweeney's.

there was far more interstate peace in the human community than war. For example, the U.S. fought Germany for six years but was at peace with her for ninety-four, with Australia for over a hundred years, with Canada for well over that, and never at war with Brazil, Norway, France, Poland, and Burma. Most people live at peace most of the time. Michael Nagler of The Metta Center for Nonviolence, suggests that we are living in the midst of a developing global peace system.[163]

The old story defined the human experience in terms of materialism, greed, and violence in a world where individuals and groups are alienated from one another and from nature. The new story is a story of belonging and of cooperative relationships. Some have called it the story of a developing "partnership society." It is the story of an emerging realization that we are a single species –humanity — living in a generous web of life that provides all we need for life. We are partnered with one another and with the earth for life. What enriches life is not mere material goods, although a minimum is surely necessary, but rather meaningful work and relationships based on trust and mutual service. Acting together we have the power to create our own destiny. We are not doomed to failure.

The Metta Center for Nonviolence holds four propositions that help define the new story:

- Life is an interconnected whole of inestimable worth.

- We cannot be fulfilled by an indefinite consumption of things, but by a potentially infinite expansion of our relationships.

- We can never injure others without injuring ourselves.

- Security does not come from... defeating "enemies"; it can only come from...turning enemies into friends.[164]

The Unprecedented Peace Revolution of Modern Times

Surprisingly, if one looks at the last 200 years of history, one sees not only the industrialization of warfare, but also a powerful trend toward a peace system and the development of a culture of peace, a veritable revolution. Beginning with the emergence of citizen-based organizations dedicated to getting rid of war in the early 19th century, some 28 trends are clearly visible leading toward a developing global peace system. These include: the emergence of international courts (starting with the International Court of Justice in 1899); the creation of international parliamentary institutions to control war (the League of Nations in 1919 and the UN in 1945); the invention of international peacekeeping forces under the auspices of the UN (Blue Helmets) and other international organizations such as the African Union, deployed in dozens of conflicts around the globe for over 50 years; the invention of nonviolent struggle as a substitute for war, beginning with Gandhi, carried on by King, perfected in the struggles to overthrow the East European Communist Empire,

---

163. https://vimeo.com/226301433

164. http://mettacenter.org/about/mission/

Marcos in the Philippines, and Mubarak in Egypt and elsewhere (even used successfully against the Nazis); the invention of new techniques of conflict resolution known as non-adversarial bargaining, mutual gains bargaining, or win-win; the development of peace research and peace education including the rapid spread of peace research institutions and projects and peace education in hundreds of colleges and universities around the world; and the peace conference movement, e.g., the Wisconsin Institute annual Student Conference and annual Fall Conference, the Peace and Justice Studies Association annual conference, the International Peace Research Association biennial conference, Pugwash annual peace conference, World BEYOND War's annual NoWar Conference, and many others.

In addition to these developments, another advancements towards a culture of peace include: a growing body of peace literature – hundreds of books, journals, and thousands of articles - and peace journalism that unpacks war propaganda in the media; the global spread of democracy (it is a fact that democracies tend not to attack one another); the development of large regions of stable peace, especially in Scandinavia, U.S./Canada/Mexico, South America, and now Western Europe—where future war is either unthinkable or highly unlikely; and the decline of racism and apartheid regimes and the end of political colonialism. We are, in fact, witnessing the end of empire. Empire is becoming an impossibility due to asymmetric warfare, nonviolent resistance, and astronomical costs that bankrupt the imperial state.

This peace revolution is enabled by the ongoing erosion of national sovereignty due to globalization; nation states can no longer keep out immigrants, ideas, economic trends, disease organisms, intercontinental ballistic missiles, and information. Further advances include the development of the worldwide women's movement; education and rights for women have been spreading rapidly in the 20th century. Educating girls is the single most important thing we can do to ensure sound economic development. Further components of the revolution are: the rise of the global environmental sustainability movement aimed at slowing and ending excessive consumption of resources and fossil fuels, which exacerbates economic injustice, climate change, and conflicts; the spread of peace-oriented forms of religion (the Christianity of Thomas Merton and Jim Wallis, the Episcopal Peace Fellowship, the Buddhism of the Dalai Lama, the Jewish Peace Fellowship, the Muslim Peace Fellowship and the Muslim Voice for Peace); and the rise of international civil society from a handful of INGOs in 1900 to tens of thousands today, creating a new, non-governmental, citizen-based world system of communication and interaction for peace, justice, environmental preservation, sustainable economic development, human rights, disease control, literacy, and clean water. The 20th and 21st centuries have also witnessed the rapid growth of an international law regime to control war, including the Geneva Conventions, the treaties banning landmines and the use of child soldiers, atmospheric testing of nuclear weapons, and placing nuclear weapons on the sea bed, among others. Further, we've seen the rise of the human rights movement, unprecedented before 1948 (the passage of the Universal Declaration of Human Rights), once totally ignored, now an international norm whose violation is an outrage in most countries and brings immediate response from states and NGOs.

Nor is this all. The peace revolution includes the rise of the global conference movement, such as the Earth Summit in 1992 in Rio, attended by 100 heads of state, 10,000 journalists, and 30,000 citizens. Since then global conferences on economic development, women, peace, global warming, and other topics have been held, creating a new forum for people from all over the world to come together to confront problems and create cooperative solutions. Globally, we have also witnessed the further evolution of a system of diplomacy with well-established norms of diplomatic immunity, 3rd party good offices, and permanent missions—all designed to allow states to communicate even in conflict situations. The development of global interactive communication via the World Wide Web and cell phones has fostered all of these advancements, by providing the means for ideas about democracy, peace, environment, and human rights to spread almost instantly. Perhaps most important is a global shift in attitudes about war, a sharp decline over the past 100 years of the old attitude that war is a glorious and noble enterprise. A special part of this new story is spreading information about the record of successful nonviolent methods of peace and justice making. The emergence of this embryonic global peace system is part of the larger development of a culture of peace.

> *"Wherever people gather for selfless ends, there is vast augmentation of their individual capacities. Something wonderful, something momentous happens. An irresistible force begins to move, which, though we may not see it, is going to change our world."*
> *- Eknath Easwaraen (Spiritual Leader)*

Planetary Citizenship: One People, One Planet, One Peace

Humans constitute a single species, Homo sapiens. While we have developed a marvelous diversity of ethnic, religious, economic, and political systems which enrich our common life, we are in fact one people living on a very fragile planet. The biosphere which supports our lives and our civilizations is extremely thin, like the skin of an apple. Within it is everything we all need to stay alive and well. We all share one atmosphere, one great ocean, one global climate, one single source of fresh water endlessly cycled around the earth, one great biodiversity. These constitute the biophysical commons on which civilization rests. It is gravely threatened by our industrial way of life, and our common task is to preserve it from destruction if we wish to live on.

Today the single most important responsibility of national governments and governing agreements at the international level is the protection of the commons. Former UN Secretary General Ban Ki-moon saw the importance of this, framed as global citizenship, and made it a cornerstone of his Global Education First Initiative (GEFI). Global Citizenship Education is also a strategic pillar of the work of UNESCO. We need to think first of the health of the global commons and only second in terms of national interest, for the latter is now totally dependent on the former.

The commons also includes the social commons, which is the condition of just peace. All must be safe if any are to be safe. The safety of any must guarantee the safety of all. A just peace is a society in which there is no fear of violent attack (war or civil war), of exploitation of one group by another, no political tyranny, where everyone's basic needs are met, and where all have the right to participate in the decisions that impact them. Just as a healthy biophysical commons requires biological diversity, a healthy social commons requires social diversity.

Photo: Pancho Ramos

Protecting the commons is best achieved by voluntary consensus so that it is a self-organizing process from below, a function of shared values and mutual respect that arise out of a sense of responsibility for the planet's well-being. When consensus is not available, when some individuals, corporations, or nations do not care about the common good, when they want to make war or degrade the environment for gain, then government is needed to protect the commons and that means laws, courts, and the police power necessary to enforce them. We have reached a stage in human and evolutionary history where the protection of the commons is necessary not only for providing a good life for humanity, but to our very survival. This means new ideas, especially the realization that we are a single planetary community. It also includes creating new associations, new forms of democratic governance and new agreements between nations to protect the commons.

War not only distracts us from this vital task, but it adds to the destruction. We will never end conflict on the planet, but conflict does not have to lead to war. We are a highly intelligent species who have already developed nonviolent methods of conflict resolution which can, and in some cases are, taking the place of violent means. We need to scale these up until we provide for common security, a world where all the children are safe and healthy, free from fear, want, and persecution, a successful human civilization resting on a healthy biosphere. One people, one planet, one peace is the essence of the new story we need to tell. It is the next stage in the progress of civilization. In order to grow and spread the culture of peace we need to reinforce several already ongoing trends.

SPREADING AND FUNDING PEACE EDUCATION AND PEACE RESEARCH

"We are at a stage in human history where we can say with confidence that we know better and more effective alternatives to war and violence."
-Patrick Hiller, Peace Scientist

For millennia we educated ourselves about war, focusing our best minds on how to win it. Just as narrow-minded historians had insisted there was no such thing as Black history or women's history, so too they argued there was no such thing as the history of peace. Humanity had failed to focus on peace until the new fields of peace research and peace education developed in the wake of the catastrophe that was World War II and accelerated in the 1980s after the world came close to nuclear annihilation. In the years since, there has been a vast increase in information about the conditions of peace.

Peace Science has emerged as an academic discipline now offered worldwide by more than 450 university programs. A myriad of peer-reviewed academic journals, textbooks, and conferences address both the theoretical and practical developments in the peacebuilding arena, as do peace research institutions like the Stockholm International Peace Research Institute or the Peace Research Institute Oslo, and professional associations like the International Peace Research Association and its regional affiliates in Africa, Asia, Europe, Latin America, and North America. Lastly the Global Peace Index, now going into its 10th year, is probably the most renowned research-based measure of peacefulness or lack thereof. The point is, Peace Science is real and here to stay.
-Give Peace Science a Chance in Diplomatic Courier165

---

165. See the full article by Patrick Hiller in the Diplomatic Courier at http://www.diplomaticourier. com/2016/07/05/give-peace-science-chance/

The United States Institute of Peace (USIP) was established by Congress in 1984 as an independent, federally-funded national security institution devoted to the nonviolent prevention and mitigation of deadly conflict abroad.[166] It sponsors events, provides education, training, and publications, including a Peacemaker's Tool Kit. Unfortunately, USIP has never been known to oppose U.S. wars. Nonetheless, the existence of USIP, and other similar institutions, is a step in the right direction of spreading understanding of peaceful alternatives.

Formal and non-formal education that supports peace is an essential component of a global security system. Developing and applying knowledge and skills in the methodologies and pedagogies of peace education is also essential to "educating the many": facilitating the learning and discourse necessary to challenging assumptions of the war system and fostering political efficacy that leads to action for system change.

Betty Reardon[167] has long maintained that one of the fundamental purposes of peace education should be the fostering of political efficacy. In essence, it is not enough to teach about peace, we must also teach for peace. Most educational campaigns in the activist world are oriented toward informing citizens about the issues and the actions they might take. While informing is essential to our task of abolishing war, we must also add to our toolkit transformative learning strategies that support worldview consideration, and the internalization of values and motivations that lead to external action.

Beyond formal education, many of us engage in non-formal peace education with adults who have deeply rooted worldviews and a generally unhealthy level of pessimism about the possibilities for abolishing war. In these circumstances, it's helpful to consider some very basic practices that might be integrated into our learning strategies. The most fundamental of transformative learning processes is reflection. Reflection is essential to our growth as human beings; to challenge assumptions; internalize values and principles; and to improve our practice as activists and peacebuilders.

As activists we rarely afford ourselves the time to reflect and learn from our experience. We subscribe to the maxim: "don't just stand there – do something!" Peace researcher Kenneth Boulding flipped this call to action on its head: "Don't do something, just stand there." Betty Reardon interpreted this to mean "even in times of crisis, reflection is a fundamental necessity to intelligent human action."[168] Most important to our work as activists is the need to learn from our experience to improve our practice and develop more effective future actions. Paulo Freire, the Brazilian popular educator and author of "Pedagogy of the Oppressed," rooted reflection in a cycle of learning and action he described as "praxis." While this praxis can work as a tool to improve our actions, it is also a tool of liberation for the oppressed. We can consider many who subscribe to the view that war is essential, inevitable, or hopelessly unchangeable, to be trapped in the oppressive grip of militarism and the war system:

166. http://www.usip.org/

167. Betty Reardon is acknowledged as one of the founders of the field of peace education.

168. Reardon, B. (2011). "Concerns, Cautions and Possibilities for Peace Education for Political Efficacy," in Critical Peace Education: Difficult Dialogue, ed. Bryan Wright and Peter Trifonas. New York, NY: Springer

"Functionally, oppression is domesticating. To no longer be prey to its force, one must emerge from it and turn upon it. This can only be done by means of the praxis: reflection and action upon the world in order to transform it."
- Paulo Freire, "Pedagogy of the Oppressed"

Learning to see the world differently requires reflection, and to become reflective practitioners requires practice. Reflective inquiry is an approach we can use to pose queries and questions to facilitate perspective taking; engage in critical consideration of systems of power; consider our ethical positions and morality; and ruminate on possibilities and preferences for the world we prefer and desire.

"The principles of peace are the same whether be it in school, at home, in the community or internationally. These are primarily about how to solve our conflicts in win-win ways, i.e., in ways that meet all peoples' needs. My kindergarten teaching was thus good training for my international peace and disarmament work. And when I am back in the classroom, I can help students see that the ideas and approaches they are using to solve their conflicts are similar to the ideas and approaches we use at the United Nations to solve international conflicts."
- Alyn Ware, 2009 Right Livelihood Award Recipient

Peace Education now embraces all levels of formal education, from kindergarten through doctoral studies.[169] The Global Campaign for Peace Education has been leading efforts to universalize peace education. It builds awareness and political support for the introduction of peace education, including non-formal education, in all schools throughout the world, and promotes the education of all teachers to teach for peace.[170] Hundreds of college campuses provide majors, minors and certificate programs in peace studies and peace education. At the university level, the Peace and Justice Studies Association[171] gathers researchers, teachers and peace activists for conferences; publishes a journal, The Peace Chronicle; and provides a resource base. Curricula and courses have multiplied and are taught as age-specific instruction at all levels. In addition, a whole new field of literature has developed including hundreds of books, articles, videos and films about peace now available to the general public.

---

169. See special issue of Peace Science Digest on Peace Education at http://communication. warpreventioninitiative.org/special-issue-peace-education/

170. The Global Campaign for Peace Education was founded at the Hague Appeal for Peace Conference in 1999. See more at: http://www.peace-ed-campaign.org

171. Peace and Justice Studies Association - PJSA: https://www.peacejusticestudies.org/. PJSA is the North American affiliate of the International Peace Research Association (IPRA): http://www.iprapeace.org/

"A culture of peace will be achieved when citizens of the world understand global problems; have the skills to resolve conflict constructively; know and live by international standards of human rights, gender and racial equality; appreciate cultural diversity; and respect the integrity of the Earth. Such learning cannot be achieved without intentional, sustained and systematic education for peace."
- Campaign Statement of the Global Campaign for Peace Education

CULTIVATING PEACE JOURNALISM

"How is the world ruled and how do wars start? Diplomats tell lies to journalists and then believe what they read."
– Karl Kraus (Poet, Playwright)

The "warist" bias we commonly see in the teaching of history also infects mainstream journalism. Too many reporters, columnists, and news anchors are stuck in the old story that war is inevitable and that it brings peace. Moreover:

> *"...in the media the "expertise" related to war and peace provided by members of the intelligentsia is very one-sided. Many of these eloquent individuals have achieved their legitimacy through academic credentials, military authority, or recognition as political commentators. Their facts, opinions, and advice on matters of war and peace shape the dominant discourse and mostly serve to uphold the status quo of a war system." (Give Peace Science a Chance in Diplomatic Courier)[172]*

There are, however, new initiatives in "peace journalism," a movement conceived by peace scholar Johan Galtung. In peace journalism, editors and writers give the reader a chance to consider nonviolent responses to conflict rather than the usual knee-jerk reaction of counter violence.[173] Peace Journalism focuses on the structural and cultural causes of violence and its impacts on actual people (rather than the abstract analysis of States), and frames conflicts in terms of their real complexity in contrast to war journalism's simple "good guys versus bad guys." It also seeks to publicize peace initiatives commonly ignored by the mainstream press. The Center for Global Peace Journalism publishes *The Peace Journalist Magazine* and offers 10 characteristics of "PJ":

1. PJ is proactive, examining the causes of conflict, and looking for ways to encourage dialogue before violence occurs.

2. PJ looks to unite parties, rather than divide them, and eschews oversimplified "us vs. them" and "good guy vs. bad guy" reporting.

---

172. See the full article by Patrick Hiller in the Diplomatic Courier at http://www.diplomaticourier. com/2016/07/05/give-peace-science-chance/

173. It is a growing movement, according to the website www.peacejournalism.org

3. Peace reporters reject official propaganda, and instead seek facts from all sources.

4. PJ is balanced, covering issues/suffering/peace proposals from all sides of a conflict.

5. PJ gives voice to the voiceless, instead of just reporting for and about elites and those in power.

6. Peace journalists provide depth and context, rather than just superficial and sensational "blow by blow" accounts of violence and conflict.

7. Peace journalists consider the consequences of their reporting.

8. Peace journalists carefully choose and analyze the words they use, understanding that carelessly selected words are often inflammatory.

9. Peace journalists thoughtfully select the images they use, understanding that they can misrepresent an event, exacerbate an already dire situation, and re-victimize those who have suffered.

10. Peace Journalists offer counter-narratives that debunk media-created or -perpetuated stereotypes, myths, and misperceptions.

The following table based on Johan Galtung's work compares the Peace Journalism framework to the War/Violence Journalism framework:[174] A notable example is Democracy Now!'s War and Peace Report. It provides the "audience with access to people and perspectives rarely heard in the U.S. corporate-sponsored media, including independent and international journalists, ordinary people from around the world who are directly affected by U.S. foreign policy, grassroots leaders and peace activists, artists, academics and independent analysts".[175]

Another example is PeaceVoice, a project of the Oregon Peace Institute.[176] PeaceVoice welcomes submission of op-eds that take a "new story" approach to international conflict and then distributes them to newspapers and blogs around the United States. Taking advantage of the internet, there are many blogs that also distribute the new paradigm thinking including Waging Nonviolence, the Transcend Media Service, New Clear Vision, Peace Action Blog, Waging Peace Blog, Bloggers for Peace and many other sites on the World Wide Web.

With growing recognition of Peace Journalism, viable alternatives to the common destructive responses in the war system will be made available to the many publics. Once those alternatives come to light, it has been proven that there will be a decline in public support for war.[177] Peace research, education, journalism and blogging are part of the newly developing culture of peace, as are recent developments in religion.

---

174. Galtung's table re-created in Lynch, Jake, and Annabel McGoldrick. 2007. "Peace Journalism." In Handbook of Peace and Conflict Studies, edited by Charles Webel and Johan Galtung, 248–64. London; New York: Routledge.

175. See www.democracynow.org

176. See www.peacevoice.info

177. See Peace Science Digest analysis Proven Decline in Public Support for War When the Alternatives Come to Light at http://communication.warpreventioninitiative.org/?p=227

Peace/Journalism	War/Violence Journalism
I.Peace/conflict oriented	I.War/violence-oriented
Explore conflict formation, x parties, y goals, z issues General 'win, win' orientation Open space, open time; causes and outcomes anywhere, also in history/ culture Making conflicts transparent Giving voice to all parties; empathy, understanding See conflict/war as problem, focus on conflict creativity Humanization of all sides Proactive: prevention before any violence/war occurs	Focus on conflict arena, 2 parties, 1 goal (win), war General zero-sum orientation Closed space, closed time; causes and exits in arena, who threw the first stone Making wars opaque/secret 'Us-them' journalism, propaganda, voice, for 'us' See 'them' as the problem, focus on who prevails in war Dehumanization of 'them' Reactive: waiting for violence before reporting Focus on invisible effects of violence (trauma and glory, damage to structure/culture
II. Truth-oriented	II. Propaganda-oriented
Expose untruths on all sides / uncover all cover-ups	Expose 'their' untruths / help 'our' cover-ups/lies
III. People-oriented	III. Elite-oriented
Focus on suffering all over; on women, the Aged, children, giving voice to voiceless Give name to all evil-doers Focus on people as peacemakers	Focus on 'our' suffering; on able bodied elite males, being their mouth-piece Give name to their evil-doers Focus on elite peacemakers
IV. Solution-oriented	IV. Victory-oriented
Peace = nonviolence + creativity Highlight peace initiatives, also to prevent more war Focus on structure, culture, the peaceful society Aftermath: resolution, reconstruction, reconciliation	Peace = victory + ceasefire Conceal peace initiative, before victory is at hand Focus on treaty, institution, the controlled society Leaving for another war, return if the old flares up again

UTILIZE RELIGION AS A TOOL FOR BUILDING PEACE

Religion is a powerful force in human society, helping to define the virtuous life and how we should behave toward each other. But in the contemporary world, religious extremism often ignites violence. Just recently we have seen an appeal to war by religious spokespersons. Christian "coach" Dave Daubenmire said recently: The only thing that is going to save Western Civilization is a more aggressive, more violent Christianity."[178] Similarly a religious advisor to U.S. President, Robert Jeffress, said just after meeting with him: "When it comes to how we should deal with evil doers, the Bible, in the book of Romans, is very clear: God has endowed rulers full power to use whatever means necessary — including war — to stop evil. In the case of North Korea, God has given Trump authority to take out Kim Jong-Un."[179]

On the other side, a statement by a Jihadi group said: "The ruling to kill the Americans and their allies -- civilians and military -- is an individual duty for every Muslim who can do it in any country in which it is possible to do it, in order to liberate the al-Aqsa Mosque and the holy mosque [Mecca] from their grip, and in order for their armies to move out of all the lands of Islam, defeated and unable to threaten any Muslim."[180]

---

178. http://www.rightwingwatch.org/post/dave-daubenmire-america-needs-a-more-violent-christianity/

179. Vox, https://www.vox.com/identities/2017/8/9/16118628/robert-jeffress-trump-god-supports-bombing-north-korea

180. https://fas.org/irp/world/para/docs/980223-fatwa.htm

These ideas only lead to relentless and vicious religious wars. Furthermore, Islam, Christianity, and Judaism all condone the concept of "Just War." In Christianity, Judaism and Islam, the doctrine of "Just War" is often used to explain why, in spite of teachings to the contrary, it is alright nevertheless to make war. It goes like this: war is a sin but, in this sinful world it is alright to make war if certain conditions are met. The list of preconditions for just war usually includes: a war can be declared only by a legitimate authority; a nation is the victim of aggression by others; all necessary means to solve the conflict peacefully have been exhausted; there must be a reasonable chance of success; the military means must be proportionate to the evil one is trying to defeat; non-combatants must not be targeted; and the end of the war should restore a more just and peaceful relationship between the parties than if the war had not been fought. This is vague language at best and it is easy to twist these criteria to rationalize war-making. For example, it is easy to falsely claim that the other side started the conflict, as Hitler did in attacking Poland in 1939. And in a more modern version, it is easy to claim that you are about to be attacked, or that the other side in the conflict is dangerously armed and so a preemptive "defensive" strike is necessary, as the U.S. did in attacking Iraq in 2003. Further, it is almost impossible to predict in advance that a war has a reasonable chance of success, or that the outcome will be better than the situation prior. Witness Libya after the NATO attack of 2011, which left the nation in chaos and civil war.

Under just war theory, a bombing raid that kills thousands of civilians can be said to meet the criteria, if civilians were not the direct targets but rather "collateral damage." And, in modern warfare, the overwhelming majority of victims are non-combatant civilians, and whether one intended it or not, they're just as dead and maimed as if one did. Honesty requires us to see just war theory as excusing murder.

Just war doctrine has been around for some 1,600 years and has not helped to end war. Especially given the conditions of modern warfare, we need to argue that there is no way to satisfy the traditional criteria that just war doctrine has always had to meet. So even if just war doctrine could somehow be compatible with the core ethical commandments of religion, it cannot be accomplished today or in the future. As World BEYOND War Co-Founder and Director David Swanson argues in *War is Never Just*, the traditional criteria are either impossible, amoral, or non-empirical, and cannot be met. Even if they could be met in some future war, that war would also have to accomplish so much good as to outweigh all the death and suffering created by the diversion of resources into militarism, plus the risk of nuclear apocalypse created by the War System, plus the environmental and political damage created. No war even in theory can meet that standard.

Therefore the faithful have no alternative except to figure out how to learn about and advocate for a process that ends war itself and replaces it with a peace system. If we cannot make war "just," then the discussion turns away from trying to, in some degree, diminish war's horrific nature, to abolition.

Intemperate statements and just war rationalizations are distortions of the core ethical teachings of the major religions. All of the world's religions contain scriptural teachings that advocate

peaceful relationships among all people. The "golden rule" is found in one form or another in them all, as in the scriptures below, as well as in the ethics of most atheists. For example:

- Christianity: Whatever you wish that men would do to you, do so to them. Matthew 7.12

- Judaism: What is hateful to you, do not do to your neighbor. Talmud, Shabbat 31a

- Islam: Not one of you is a believer until he loves for his brother what he loves for himself. Forty Hadith of an-Nawawi 13

- Hinduism: One should not behave towards others in a way which is disagreeable to oneself. This is the essence of morality. Mahabharata, Anusasana Parva 113.8

- Buddhism: Comparing oneself to others in such terms as "Just as I am so are they, just as they are so am I," he should neither kill nor cause others to kill. Sutta Nipata 705

- African Traditional: One going to take a pointed stick to pinch a baby bird should first try it on himself to feel how it hurts. Yoruba Proverb (Nigeria)

- Confucianism: Do not do to others what you do not want them to do to you." Analects 15.23

Many religions host organizations for peace such as the Episcopal Peace Fellowship, Pax Christi, the Jewish Voice for Peace, Muslims For Peace, the Buddhist Peace Fellowship, Yakjah (a Hindu peace organization working in the Kashmir), and the Tanenbaum Center for Interreligious Understanding. Many interfaith peace organizations are also thriving, including the Fellowship of Reconciliation (established in 1915), United Religions Initiative, Religions for Peace USA, and Multi-faith Voices for Peace and Justice. The World Council of Churches is heading up a campaign to abolish nuclear weapons.

In his humane approach to world peace the Buddhist spiritual leader Dalai Lama advocates loving kindness. In the build-up to military intervention in Syria, Pope Francis made a compelling appeal for seeking a peaceful resolution. During the 2011 Egyptian Revolution Nevin Zaki captured and tweeted the powerful image of Christians joining hands in a circle to protect a Muslim group of protesters as they prayed.

In 2007, Muslim leaders reached out to Christians in an appeal for peace in their letter "A Common Word Between Us and You."[181] In the spring of 2015, the Vatican hosted the conference "Nonviolence and Just Peace: Contributing to the Catholic Understanding of and Commitment to Nonviolence." Eighty participants concluded that the just war doctrine should be rejected as a viable or productive Catholic tradition.[182] These are just a few snapshots of a larger trend of growing advocacy of peace messages in all major religions.

Throughout the history of nonviolence, we have seen the importance of faith communities, recognizing that many nonviolent leaders are people of strong religious and moral faith. Just consider this simple quote by Catholic writer and peace advocate Thomas Merton: "War is the kingdom of Satan. Peace is the kingdom of God."

Regardless of one's faith tradition, whether rejection of institutional religion, spiritual

---

181. http://www.acommonword.com/the-acw-document/

182. See the insightful article, "*Did the Vatican just throw out its just war doctrine*" by Erica Chenoweth at https://politicalviolenceataglance.org/2016/04/19/did-the-vatican-just-throw-out-its-just-war-doctrine/

direction, or complete atheism, the work by peaceful religious initiatives is encouraging, and should be further encouraged, if only as a matter of sensible pragmatism.

THE DECLARATION OF PEACE

A faith-based declaration of peace emphasizing planetary citizenship.

These are self-evident truths:

That all humans are a single family living on a fragile and endangered planet whose life support systems must remain intact if we are to survive;

That the well-being of the planet and the well-being of humanity are one and the same;

That the well-being of each requires the well-being of all—security is common;

That all humans have a natural right to peace and a healthy planet;

That all war is a crime against humanity and nature;

That any war anywhere degrades the quality of life for all of us everywhere;

That we live at the decisive moment in history when we will choose between break down or breakthrough on a planetary scale;

That we here now dedicate our intellectual, spiritual and material resources to the establishment of permanent peace and the conservation of nature, and,

That we are fully endowed by our Creator with the wisdom and the ability to achieve these ends.

17 May, 2017 at Tomidhu Cottage, Crathie, Scotland,

Kent Drummond Shifferd

(World BEYOND War Coordinating Committee member and original co-author of "A Global Security System: An Alternative to War.")

ACCELERATING THE TRANSITION: BUILDING THE WORLD BEYOND WAR MOVEMENT

What we have outlined as the Alternative Global Security System is more than a concept; it lays out the foundation for World BEYOND War, a global, grassroots network of volunteers, activists, and allied organizations advocating for war abolition and the establishment of a just and sustainable peace. We follow a two-pronged approach of peace education and nonviolent direct action organizing to dispel the myths of war, educate about its alternatives, and advocate for structural and cultural change. The strength of our movement depends on having a diversity of support from people all over the world coming together for a singular cause: peace. To that end, over 500 organizations and 75,000 individuals from 158 countries have signed our Declaration of Peace, pledging to work nonviolently for a World BEYOND War.[183] Our decentralized, volunteer-run structure, consisting of World BEYOND War chapters and affiliated groups around the world, is designed to facilitate global collaboration and bottom-up decision-making.

The World BEYOND War Declaration of Peace

I understand that wars and militarism make us less safe rather than protect us, that they kill, injure and traumatize adults, children and infants, severely damage the natural environment, erode civil liberties, and drain our economies, siphoning resources from life-affirming activities. I commit to engage in and support nonviolent efforts to end all war and preparations for war and to create a sustainable and just peace.

In building a movement for war abolition, our work addresses the entire institution of war, setting us apart from past models that opposed only specific weapons or a particular war on the grounds that it isn't being run well or isn't as proper as some other war. Through our education programs and advocacy campaigns, we shift the moral dialogue by making the case that the institution of war should be viewed as tantamount to mass-murder, even when that mass-murder is accompanied by flags or music or assertions of authority and promotion of irrational fear. We expand the focus of peace activism beyond the harm that wars cause to the aggressors, in order to fully acknowledge and appreciate the suffering of all.

In working towards global war abolition, the elephant in the room is the United States government, which, at $1 trillion a year, accounts for half of global annual military spending. Because of the proliferation of U.S.-led wars and the global spread of U.S. foreign military bases, our work squarely acknowledges the U.S.'s primary role as global warmonger and

---

183. Sign the Declaration of Peace at www.worldbeyondwar.org/individual

aims to engage citizens everywhere, not just U.S. residents, in a campaign to demilitarize the world's largest war machine. While ending U.S. war-making wouldn't eliminate war globally, it would eliminate the pressure that is driving several other nations to increase their military spending. It would deprive NATO of its leading advocate for and greatest participant in wars. It would cut off the largest supply of weapons to Western Asia (a.k.a. the Middle East) and other regions. It would remove the major barrier to reconciliation and reunification of Korea. It would create U.S. willingness to support arms treaties, join the International Criminal Court, and allow the United Nations to move in the direction of its stated purpose of eliminating war. It would create a world free of nations threatening first-use of nukes, and a world in which nuclear disarmament might proceed more rapidly. Gone would be the last major nation using cluster bombs or refusing to ban landmines. If the United States kicked the war habit, war itself would suffer a major and possibly fatal setback.

A focus on U.S. war preparations cannot work in isolation without similar efforts everywhere. Numerous nations are investing, and even increasing their investments, in war. All militarism must be opposed. And victories for a peace system tend to spread by example. When the British Parliament opposed attacking Syria in 2013, it influenced the U.S. to follow suit and nix its proposal for war. In January 2014 in Havana, Cuba, when 31 nations committed to never making use of war, those voices were heard in other nations of the world.[184]

COALITION-BUILDING

Our holistic approach prioritizes multilateral coalition-building, or "fusion organizing." This involves building cross-sector collaborations with those that ought to oppose the military industrial complex due to its widespread social and ecological impact: environmentalists, the faith community, ethicists, public health advocates, mental health professionals, economists, journalists, historians, labor unions, civil libertarians, internationalists and world travelers, and good government groups. Additionally, there are opportunities for partnership with proponents of measures that could be funded if war dollars were re-allocated, such as advocates for education, healthcare, housing, arts, science, and infrastructure reform. This broad-based coalition work aims to overcome a common issue in activist circles of working in "single-issue silos." The Alternative Global Security System (AGSS) offers a unifying language wherein different social movement organizations can align, without losing their organizational or movement identity.

Multi-track diplomacy is a systems-based approach to peacebuilding developed and put into practice by Louise Diamond and Ambassador (Ret.) John W. McDonald. Multi-track diplomacy reflects the idea that international exchanges can take many forms beyond official negotiations between diplomats. Examples of multi-track diplomacy include official and unofficial conflict resolution efforts, citizen and scientific exchanges, international business negotiations, international cultural and athletic activities and other international contacts and

---

184. See more on the Community of Latin American and Caribbean states at: http://www.nti.org/treaties-and-regimes/community-latin-american-and-caribbean-states-celac/

A Global Security System: An Alternative to War 2018-19 Edition

cooperative efforts. Nine specific tracks which produce a synergy in peacebuilding are: public opinion and communication, government, professional conflict resolution, business, private citizens, activism, religion, funding, and research, training and education.[185] The appealing factor in such a system is that all actors have a role to play in advancing peace. This allows for them to individually and collectively bring their strengths into a larger system, empowering the whole. It comes down to the simple idea that not everyone can be all things to all people, but that everyone has a role to play.

PEACE EDUCATION PROGRAMS

Peace education is one prong of our two-step approach to change-making. Education is a critical component of an alternative global security system and an essential tool for getting us there. Our programs educate both *about* and *for* the abolition of war. Our educational resources are based on knowledge and research that expose the myths of war and illuminate the proven nonviolent, peaceful alternatives that can bring us authentic security. We encourage participants in our programs to reflect upon critical questions and engage in dialogue with peers toward challenging assumptions of the war system. These forms of critical, reflective learning have been well documented to support increased political efficacy and action for system change.

World BEYOND War offers numerous tools and resources for engaged learning, in addition to this annual publication, which is available in print, e-book, PDF, and audio formats. Our educational resources are designed to be distributed widely to popularize support for war abolition. To that end, we work with volunteers in our network worldwide to organize World BEYOND War book clubs, discussion groups, film series, and guest lectures. Our website, WorldBeyondWar.org, serves as a free information hub for the war abolition movement. It houses militarism maps, charts, graphics, arguments, talking points, articles, and videos to help people make the case that wars can, should, and must be abolished. Each section of the website includes lists of relevant books and films, and links to external resources. We also offer online courses, a free educational webinar series, a Speakers Bureau, and "Study War No More," a free online study and discussion guide that accompanies this book. Bolstering our educational efforts is our global billboard project. Funded primarily by small-dollar donors, our roadside billboards, bus shelter posters, and subway advertisements amplify the war abolition message in the public eye.

Study War No More is an online learning tool developed in partnership with the Global Campaign for Peace Education. The guide can be used for independent study or as a tool for facilitating dialogue and discussion in classrooms (secondary, university) and with community groups. Each discussion topic features a video introduction from our "study and action partners" – leading global thinkers, strategists, academics, advocates and activists who are already developing components of an alternative global security system. The guide can be accessed at globalsecurity.worldbeyondwar.org.

---

185. Diamond, Louise, & McDonald, John W. (1993). Multi-track diplomacy: a systems approach to peace (Rev. ed.). Washington, DC: Institute for Multi-Track Diplomacy.

Online Courses

World BEYOND War offers facilitated online courses led by experts, and allied activists and changemakers from around the world. Past offerings have included:

War Abolition 101: How We Create a Peaceful World
How can we make the best argument for shifting from war to peace? How can we become more effective advocates and activists for ending particular wars, ending all wars, pursuing disarmament, and creating systems that maintain peace?

War Abolition 201: Building the Alternative Global Security System
With what do we replace the war system (aka the military-industrial-corporate-governmental complex)? What truly makes us secure? What are the moral, social, political, philosophical and pragmatic foundations of an alternative global security system – a system in which peace is pursued by peaceful means? What actions and strategies might we pursue in building this system? War Abolition 201 explores these questions and more with the goal of engaging students in learning that leads to action.

The aim of our education programs is to shift the narrative about war so that talk of a "good war" will sound no more plausible than a "benevolent rape" or "philanthropic slavery" or "virtuous child abuse." Our education programs foster a culture of peace in which war resisters, conscientious objectors, peace advocates, diplomats, whistleblowers, journalists, nonviolent activists, and human shields are society's true heroes.

Our materials use common language and appeal to shared values that make the alternative global security system palatable to the public at large. At the same time, we move beyond mainstream western peace symbolism, such as the peace sign, doves, olive branches, and people holding hands. These cliché symbols, while non-contentious, fail to communicate tangible meanings of peace. Rather, the AGSS offers a new vocabulary and vision of realistic alternatives to war and paths toward common security. We use the framework of world citizenship to advance popular thinking beyond patriotism, nationalism, xenophobia, racism, religious bigotry, and exceptionalism. In this way, the alternative global security system is cross-cultural and transnational.

Global solidarity in educational efforts constitutes an important part of the education itself. Student and cultural exchanges between the West and nations on the Pentagon's likely target list (Syria, Iran, North Korea, China, and Russia) can foster peace-building and strengthen people's resistance towards their governments waging wars. Similar exchanges between nations investing in war and nations that have ceased to do so, or which do so at a greatly reduced scale, can be of great value as well.[186] In the film *The Ultimate Wish: Ending the*

---

186. Peace Scientist Patrick Hiller found in his research that traveling abroad led U.S. citizens to better recognize U.S. privilege and perception around the world, to understand how perceived enemies are dehumanized in the U.S. main narrative, to see 'the other' in a positive way, to reduce

A Global Security System: An Alternative to War 2018-19 Edition

Nuclear Age, we see a survivor of Nagasaki meeting a survivor of Auschwitz. In watching their interaction, one does not remember or care which nation committed which horror. A peace culture will see all war with that same clarity. War is an abomination not because of who commits it but because of what it is.

NONVIOLENT DIRECT ACTION CAMPAIGNS

Our strategic war abolition campaign is broken down into short-term and intermediate advocacy goals, understood as partial steps along the way towards replacing the war system. These goals are accomplished through nonviolent direct action organizing campaigns, which include weapons divestment, counter-recruitment, close bases, and global justice. These campaigns operate in tandem to our peace education programs, serving both as tools for policy change and continued education and awareness-building. As a hub for educational campaign materials, organizing training, and promotional assistance, World BEYOND War teams up with activists, volunteers, and allied groups to plan, promote, and amplify pro-peace campaigns worldwide.

Weapons Divestment: World BEYOND War is a founding member of the Divest from the War Coalition. Through grassroots campaigns worldwide, the coalition works to divest individual, institutional, and government funds from weapons manufacturing corporations and military contractors, and advocates for socially responsible reinvestment alternatives.

Counter-Recruitment: This campaign counters military recruiting in schools by advocating for increased transparency and expanded avenues for opting out of recruitment. Designed for the U.S., the campaign can be scaled up and tailored to counter country-specific recruitment. In the U.S., campaign goals include passing state-level "opt-out" legislation to better inform parents of their legal right to opt their children out of recruitment, and shutting down JROTC marksmanship programs in high schools. As of 2018, Maryland is the only U.S. state with strong "opt-out" legislation on the books.

Close Bases: This campaign aims to raise public awareness and organize nonviolent mass resistance against military bases around the world, with particular emphasis on U.S. foreign military bases, which constitute 95% of all foreign military bases worldwide. Foreign military bases are centers of warmongering and expansionism, causing severe environmental, economic, political, and health impacts on local populations. World BEYOND War is a founding member in the Coalition Against U.S. Foreign Military Bases.

Global Justice & The Rule of Law: This policy-oriented campaign petitions governments to abide by international law. It calls for the ratification of the amendment to the Rome Statute on the prosecution of the crime of aggression, compulsory jurisdiction of the International Court of Justice, and the prosecution of all war crimes at the International Criminal Court.

Pass Resolutions: A tactic in our war abolition campaign is to pass local and state or provincial

prejudices and stereotypes, and to create empathy.

level resolutions calling for the reallocation of military spending to human and environmental needs. Together with our allies, we have helped pass resolutions in numerous localities to demand a decrease in government spending on war and preparations for war.

Direct action organizing involves building our strength in numbers and then utilizing that people power en masse to put targeted pressure on decision makers, such as elected officials, institutional heads, or corporate executives, to urge them to make the policy changes that we want to see. To this end, organizing requires constant outreach to individuals and allied organizations to take collective action. Each campaign area employs varied tactics, offering activists numerous avenues for engagement. Campaign tactics include, but are not limited to, collecting petition signatures; phone banking; organizational and elected official sign-on letters; writing letters-to-the-editor and op-eds; social media campaigning; meeting with elected officials and other decision-makers; and organizing nonviolent, Gandhian-style protests, sit-ins, and marches. Tactics can vary in type and intensity in accordance with the strategy needed to sway a decision-maker to achieve the campaign's goal. Organizations like Campaign Nonviolence and the International Center on Nonviolent Conflict examine the use of nonviolent direct action and conflict escalation worldwide and create trainings for activists and organizers based on insights from practice and research.

CONCLUSION

War is always a choice, and it is always a bad choice. It is a choice that always leads to more war. It is not mandated in our genes or our human nature. It is not the only possible response to conflicts. Nonviolent action is a more effective choice because it defuses and helps resolve conflict. But the choice for nonviolence must not wait until conflict erupts. It must be built into society: built into institutions for conflict forecasting, mediation, adjudication, and peacekeeping. It must be built into education in the form of knowledge, perceptions, beliefs and values—in short, a culture of peace. Societies consciously prepare far in advance for the war response and so perpetuate insecurity. Why would humans continue on this path? Even pre-conflict prevention is more effective and less costly than post-conflict conflict protection. In other words, preventing war is less costly than cleaning up after war. And that does not even include the human suffering and trauma that can be avoided.

Some powerful groups benefit from war and violence. The vast majority of humans, however, will gain a lot from a World BEYOND War.

For peace to prevail, we must prepare equally far in advance for the better choice. If you want peace, prepare for peace.

> *"Forget that this task of planet-saving is not possible in the time required. Don't be put off by people who know what is not possible. Do what needs to be done, and check to see if it was impossible only after you are done."*
> *- Paul Hawken (Environmentalist, Author)*

BE INSPIRED

- In less than three years, over 75,000 people and 500 organizations from 158 countries have signed World BEYOND War's pledge for peace.

- Demilitarization is underway. Costa Rica and 24 other countries have disbanded their militaries altogether.

- European nations, which had fought each other for over a thousand years, including the horrendous world wars of the twentieth century, now work collaboratively in the European Union.

- Former advocates of nuclear weapons, including former U.S. Senators and Secretaries of State and numerous retired, high-ranking military officers, have publicly rejected nuclear weapons and called for their abolition.

- There is a massive, worldwide movement to end the carbon economy and hence the wars over oil.

- Many thoughtful people and organizations around the world are calling for an end to the counterproductive "war on terror."

- Over one million organizations in the world are actively working toward peace, social justice, and environmental protection.

- Thirty-one Latin American and Caribbean nations created a zone of peace on January 29, 2014.

- In the last 100 years, we humans have created for the first time in history institutions and movements to control international violence: the UN, the World Court, the International Criminal Court; and treaties such as the Kellogg-Briand Pact, the Treaty to Ban Landmines, the Treaty to Ban Child Soldiers, and many others.

- In 2017, the Treaty on the Prohibition on Nuclear Weapons was adopted by the United Nations

- A peace revolution is already underway.

APPENDICES

WHO WE ARE

World BEYOND War is a global nonviolent movement to end war and establish a just and sustainable peace. World BEYOND War began January 1, 2014. It was Co-Founded by David Hartsough and David Swanson.

Staff (as of July 2018)

> Director: David Swanson
>
> Education Coordinator: Tony Jenkins
>
> Organizing Director: Greta Zarro

Volunteers

> The articles and videos on our website are updated by Donnal Walter and Marc Eliot Stein
>
> The events map on this website is updated by Ellen Thomas

World Beyond War is run by committees, which are constantly looking for new members. Please let us know if you'd like to join.

Coordinating Committee (as of July 2018)

> Leah Bolger, Chair — U.S.
>
> David Swanson — U.S.
>
> Kent Shifferd — U.S.
>
> Alice Slater — U.S.
>
> Odile Hugonot Haber — U.S.
>
> Robert Fantina — Canada
>
> Dave Webb — U.K.
>
> Ellen Thomas — U.S.
>
> Barry Sweeney — Ireland
>
> Gar Smith — U.S.
>
> Ingrid Style — Canada
>
> Donnal Walter — U.S.
>
> Pat Elder — U.S.
>
> Marc Eliot Stein — U.S.
>
> Liz Remmerswaal Hughes — New Zealand.

World BEYOND War Advisory Board

> Mairead Maguire
>
> Kathy Kelly
>
> Kevin Zeese

Maria Santelli

Hakim

Gareth Porter

Ann Wright

Medea Benjamin

Johan Galtung

David Hartsough

John Vechey

Patrick Hiller

Matthew Hoh

Emanuel Pastreich

Contact World BEYOND War

Email us: info@worldbeyondwar.org,

Write us: World BEYOND War, P.O. Box 1484, Charlottesville VA 22902 USA.

Support our Work

We are a people-powered movement; we never take money from corporations or governments. We rely on small-dollar donations from individuals in our global, grassroots network. Please support our work by sending a one-time donation or becoming a monthly sustainer for $9 or more a month (donations are tax-deductible in the U.S.).

Make U.S. checks payable to World BEYOND War/AFGJ.

Send donations by check to: World BEYOND War, PO Box 1484, Charlottesville, VA 22902 USA
Donate online using a credit card here: https://worldbeyondwar.org/donate/

Donors

Special thanks to our recurring donors and to:

> The Puffin Foundation
>
> Christopher and LuAnne Hormel of the Fire Monkey Fund of RSF Social Finance
>
> Home Rule Globally
>
> John Vechey
>
> Jubitz Family Foundation
>
> Wallace Action Fund
>
> Peaceworkers
>
> Stephen Clemens
>
> Angeliki V. Keil
>
> Deb Sawyer
>
> Wayne Martinson
>
> Medea Benjamin
>
> Peter Selby
>
> Josh Mitteldorf
>
> Robert Barkley
>
> Paddy Welles
>
> William McLaughlin
>
> Nancy Weaver
>
> Arthur Milholland
>
> Robin Lloyd
>
> Helen Alexander

WORLD BEYOND WAR CHAPTERS, AFFILIATES AND COUNTRY COORDINATORS

*List as of August 1, 2018. New chapters and affiliates are added weekly.

*Links to chapter websites and contacts can be found on our website:
https://worldbeyondwar.org/findchapter/

Afghanistan

> Affiliate: Rehabilitee Organization for Afghan War Victims

Australia

> Affiliate: Wage Peace

Affiliate: Hunter Peace Group

Cameroon

> Chapter: World Beyond War – Cameroon

Canada

    Country Coordinator: Bob Fantina

    Chapter: World Beyond War – Toronto

    Affiliate: Canadian Peace Initiative

    Affiliate: Anutek Developments Inc.

    Affiliate: World Without Fear

    Affiliate: Toronto Raging Grannies

Chile

    Affiliate: Movimiento Todos Por La Paz

Democratic Republic of the Congo

    Affiliate: CongoInThePicture

Denmark

    Affiliate: Food Not Bombs

Deutschland

    Country Coordinator: Heinrich Buecker

    Affiliate: Initiative of order people for peace

England

    Affiliate: Save The Earth Cooperative

    Affiliate: Commonweal: For a Nonviolent World

France

    Affiliate: Survival

Ghana

    Affiliate: Anam Foundation for Peace Building

Ireland

    Country Coordinator: Barry Sweeney

Italia

    Country Coordinators: Patrick Boylan

Japan

    Country Coordinator: Joseph Essertier

Korea

    Country Coordinator: Emanuel Yi Pastreich

    Mandarin Language Coordinator

Nepal

    Affiliate: Charumati Buddhist Mission

Netherlands

       Country Coordinator: Muhumuza Valentin Akayezu

New Zealand

       Country Coordinator: Liz Remmerswaal Hughes

       Chapter: Hawke's Bay

Nigeria

       Country Coordinator: Oluwafemi Temitope

       Affiliate: Smiles Africa International Youth Development Initiative

       Affiliate: International Youth Reformation Organization

       Affiliate: World Youth Peace Organization

       Affiliate: War Orphans & Widows Development Centre

       Affiliate: Centre for Convention on Democratic Integrity

Pakistan

       Affiliate: Youth Association for Development

       Affiliate: Association for Integrated Development Balochistan

Puerto Rico

       Country Coordinator: Myrna Pagán

Singapore

       Country Coordinator: Dr. Wee Teck Young (known by Afghan youth as "Hakim")

South Africa

       Country Coordinator: Terry Crawford-Browne

Sweden

       Country Coordinator: Agneta Norberg

       Affiliate: Swedish Peace Council

Tunisia

Country Coordinator: Gamra Zenaidi

Uganda

       Affiliate: Peace Choice Uganda

United States

       Country Coordinator: David Swanson

       Affiliate: The #PeaceSalon – Virtual weekly peace gathering hosted by #TripForPeace

Arkansas

       Affiliate: Arkansas Coalition for Peace and Justice (ACPJ)

       Affiliate: Arkansas Nonviolence Alliance

California

       Affiliate: Veterans For Peace, Chapter 71, Sonoma

Affiliate: Code Pink Golden Gate

Affiliate: NatureConnect

Affiliate: Threads of Peace, Inc.

Affiliate: Monterey Peace and Justice Center

Affiliate: Los Angeles Institute of Noetic Sciences

Affiliate: Chico Peace and Justice Center: Confronting Endless War

Affiliate: Peace Fresno

Colorado

Affiliate: The Colorado Coalition for Prevention of Nuclear War

Connecticut

Affiliate: CT Peace and Solidarity Coalition

Affiliate: The Educational Community, Inc.

DC

Affiliate: National Campaign for a Peace Tax Fund

Affiliate: Global Zero: DC Metro

Florida

Chapter: World Beyond War – Central Florida

Affiliate: Veterans For Peace Chapter 14 Gainesville

Affiliate: Veterans for Peace Jax

Affiliate: Peacehome Campaigns

Illinois

Affiliate: Chicago Veterans For Peace

Affiliate: West Suburban Faith-Based Peace Coalition

Michigan

Affiliate: American Action for Peace in Yemen

Minnesota

Affiliate: Veterans For Peace Chapter 27

Affiliate: Minnesota Peace Project

Montana

Affiliate: Jeannette Rankin Peace Center

New Hampshire

Affiliate: #Resist: Hillsborough County

New Mexico

Affiliate: Future Vision Coaching

New York

> Affiliate: Pax Christi Metro New York
>
> Affiliate: Cornell Nuclear Disarmament Group
>
> Affiliate: Global Warming Is Real
>
> Affiliate: Veterans For Peace – NYC Chapter 034
>
> Affiliate: Veterans For Peace – Saratoga Springs 147
>
> Affiliate: PeaceWorks!
>
> Affiliate: Gratitude to Water Catholic Workers
>
> Affiliate: Long Island for Peace

North Carolina

> Affiliate: Quaker House
>
> Affiliate: Veterans For Peace Chapter 099 Asheville

Ohio

> Affiliate: World 5.0

Oklahoma

> Affiliate: Norman Peace and Justice Center

Oregon

> Affiliate: Veterans For Peace, Linus Pauling Chapter

Pennsylvania

> Affiliate: Earth Rights Institute

Texas

> Affiliate: Border Peace Presence El Paso, TX

Vermont

> Affiliate: World Beyond War – Burlington

Virginia

> Affiliate: The Oracle Institute & Peace Pentagon HUB

Washington

> Chapter: World Beyond War – Seattle
>
> Chapter: World Beyond War – Tri Cities
>
> Affiliate: No More Bombs
>
> Affiliate: Veterans For Peace, Greater Seattle Chapter 92
>
> Affiliate: Veterans for Peace 109, Olympia
>
> Affiliate: Grassroots ACTION Whatcom
>
> Affiliate: Veterans For Peace Chapter 035 Spokane
>
> Affiliate: Roots of Conflict

Wisconsin

Affiliate: Peace Action Wisconsin

Wales

Affiliate: Learn With Grandma

In the UK? Join the Movement for the Abolition of War.

RESOURCE GUIDE

"Study War No More" - WBW's Study & Action Guide for this book! - http://globalsecurity. worldbeyondwar.org/

Peace Almanac - http://worldbeyondwar.org/calendar/

Mapping Militarism - https://worldbeyondwar.org/militarism-mapped/

Where Your Income Tax Money Really Goes- https://www.warresisters.org/resources/pie-chart-flyers-where-your-income-tax-money-really-goes

Peace Science Digest - www.peacesciencedigest.org

Global Peace Index - http://www.visionofhumanity.org/

National Priorities Project, Military / Security - https://www.nationalpriorities.org/works-on/military-security/

The Seville Statement on Violence - http://www.unesco.org/cpp/uk/declarations/seville.pdf

Rotarian Action Group for Peace, Peace Map - https://fortress.maptive.com/ver4/26293cafb7ba975828856262b4d1ad3e

BOOKS

Ackerman, Peter, and Jack DuVall, A Force More Powerful: A Century of Nonviolent Conflict (2000).

American Friends Service Committee, Shared Security: Reimagining U.S. Foreign Policy. (https://afsc.org/sites/ afsc.civicactions.net/files/documents/shared-security_web.pdf)

Amster, Randall, Peace Ecology (2014).

Bacevich, Andrew, The new American militarism: how Americans are seduced by war (2005).

Bacevich, Andrew, Washington rules: America's path to permanent war (2010).

Beckwith, Kathy, A Mighty Case Against War: What America Missed in U.S. History Class and What We (All) Can Do Now (2016).

Benjamin, Medea, & Evans, Jodie, Stop the next war now: effective responses to violence and terrorism (2005).

Boulding, Elise, and Randall Forsberg, Abolishing War: Cultures and Institutions (1998).

Boulding, Elise, Cultures of Peace: The Hidden Side of History (2000).

Boyle, Francis Anthony, Defending Civil Resistance Under International Law (1987).

Buchheit, Paul, American Wars: Illusions and Realities (2008).

Burrowes, Robert J. The Strategy of Nonviolent Defense: A Gandhian Approach (1996).

Cady, Duane L., From Warism to Pacifism: A Moral Continuum (2010).

Chappell, Paul, The Art of Waging Peace (2013).

Chenoweth, Erica, and Maria J. Stephan, Why Civil Resistance Works: The Strategic Logic of Nonviolent Conflict (2011).

Delgado, Sharon, Shaking the Gates of Hell: Faith-led Resistance to Corporate Globalization (2007).

Diamond, Louise, and John W. McDonald, Multi-track diplomacy: a systems approach to peace (1993).

Dower, John W., Cultures of War: Pearl Harbor / Hiroshima / 9-11 / Iraq (2010).

Elder, Pat, Military Recruiting in the United States (2016)

Elworthy, Scilla, Peace is Now Possible: The Business Plan to Build a World Without War (2017)

Engler, Mark, and Paul Engler. This is an Uprising: How Nonviolent Revolt is Shaping the Twenty-First Century (2016)

Faure-Brac, Russell, Transition to Peace: A Defense Engineer's Search for an Alternative to War (2012).

Fazal, Anwar, and Lakshmi Menon. The Right Livelihood Way: A Sourcebook for Changemakers (2016)

Fry, Douglas, War, peace, and human nature: the convergence of evolutionary and cultural views (2013).

Galtung, Johan. Abolishing War. Criminalizing War, Removing War Causes, Removing War as Institution (accessed 2016).

Galtung, Johan. A Theory Of Peace. Building Direct-Structural-Cultural Peace (accessed 2016).

Goldstein, Joshua S., Winning the War on War: The Decline of Armed Conflict Worldwide (2011).

Grossman, Dave, On Killing: The Psychological Cost of Learning to Kill in War and Society (1996).

Hand, Judith L., Shift: The Beginning of War, the Ending of War (2014).

Harris, Ian, and Mary Lee Morrison, Peace Education, 3rd ed., (2012).

Hartsough, David, Waging Peace: Global Adventures of a Lifelong Activist (2014).

Hastings, Tom, Ecology of War and Peace: Counting Costs of Conflict (2000).

Hastings, Tom, A New Era of Nonviolence. The Power of Civil Society over War (2014).

Hathaway, Oona, and Scott Shapiro. The Internationalists: How a Radical Plan to Outlaw War Remade the World (2017).

Hawken, Paul, Blessed Unrest: How the Largest Movement in the World Came into Being and Why No One Saw It Coming (2007).

Irwin, Robert A., Building a Peace System (1989; free online via HathiTrust).

Kaldor, Mary, Global Civil Society: An Answer to War (2003).

Kelly, Kathy, Other Lands Have Dreams: From Baghdad to Pekin Prison (2005).

Lederach, John Paul, The Moral Imagination: The Art and Soul of Building Peace (2005).

Mahoney, Liam, and Luis Enrique Eguren, Unarmed Bodyguards: International Accompaniment for the Protection of Human Rights (1997).

Marr, Andrew, Tools for Peace: The Spiritual Craft of St. Benedict and Rene Girard (2007).

Mische, Patricia M., and Melissa Merkling, eds., Toward a Global Civilization? The Contribution of Religions (2001).

Myers, Winslow, Living Beyond War. A Citizen's Guide (2009).

Nagler, Michael, The Search for a Nonviolent Future (2004).

Nelson-Pallmeyer, Jack, Authentic Hope: It's the End of the World As We Know It But Soft Landings Are Possible (2012).

Pilisuk Marc, and Jennifer Achord Rountree, The Hidden Structure of Violence: Who Benefits from Global Violence and War (2015).

O'Dea, James, Cultivating Peace: Becoming a 21st-Century Peace Ambassador (2012).

Ricigliano, Rob, Making Peace Last: A Toolbox for Sustainable Peacebuilding (2012).

Schwartzberg, Joseph E., Transforming the United Nations System (2013).

Sharp, Gene, Waging Nonviolent Struggle (2005).

Sharp, Gene, The Politics of nonviolent Action (1973).

Sharp, Gene, Civilian-Based Defense: A Post-Military Weapons System (1990) available at http://www.aeinstein.org/wp-content/uploads/2013/09/Civilian-Based-Defense-English.pdf

Shifferd, Kent, From War to Peace: A Guide to the Next Hundred Years (2011).

Solomon, Norman. War Made Easy: How Presidents and Pundits Keep Spinning Us to Death. (2010).

Somlai, Anton, Peace Vigil: Living Without Hesitation (2009).

Swanson, David, War No More: The Case for Abolition (2013).

Swanson, David, When the World Outlawed War (2011).

Swanson, David, War Is A Lie (2nd Ed., 2016).

Thompson, J. Milburn, Justice & Peace: A Christian Primer (2003).

Vine, David. Base Nation: How U.S. Military Bases Abroad Harm America and the World. (2015)

Williams, Jody, Goose, Stephen., & Wareham, Mary. Banning landmines: disarmament, citizen diplomacy, and human security (2008).

MOVIES

     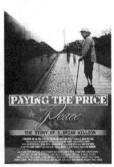

A Bold Peace

A Force More Powerful

Bringing Down a Dictator

Orange Revolution

Pray the Devil Back to Hell

Paying the Price of Peace

DEBUNKING MYTHS OF WAR (HANDOUT)

War gains support and acceptance from widespread belief in false information, and the accumulation of false information into generally false concepts or myths about war. This is good news, because it means we are not intractably divided by ideology or worldview. Rather, we will find more widespread agreement about war if we can just achieve more widespread awareness of accurate information.

World BEYOND War's maintains a list of common war myths and the facts that debunk them. We challenge several myths that fall under the following categories – War is 1) inevitable, 2) necessary, 3) beneficial, and 4) just.

Following is an abbreviated myth and fact answer sheet that is great for talking points and leading a basic discussion. You can find our full-length arguments here: https://worldbeyondwar.org/myths/

Myth: It is impossible to eliminate war.

Fact: to say this is to submit fatalistically to determinism, to believe that we humans do not make our history but are the helpless victims of forces beyond our control, that we have no free will. In fact, it was once said that it was impossible to abolish legalized slavery, dueling, blood feuds and other institutions that were deeply embedded in societies of their time, practices that are now, if not fully in the dustbin of history, universally understood to be eliminable. War is a social invention, not a permanent feature of human existence. It is a choice, not something imposed by a law of nature.

Myth: War is in our genes.

Fact: if this were true, all societies would be making war all of the time, which we know is not the case. During the most recent 6,000 years, war has been sporadic and some societies have not known war. Some have known it and then abandoned it. Quite a few nations have chosen to have no military. War is a social, not a biological event.

Myth: War is "natural."

Fact: it is very difficult to get people to kill in warfare. A great deal of psychological conditioning is required even to get them to fire their guns and very often they are traumatized by the experience and suffer post-traumatic stress disorder. Many veterans of combat end up chemically dependent and many commit suicide, unable to live with what they have done. Mass killing is not a part of our nature—quite the opposite is true.

Myth: We have always had war.

Fact: war is an invention of the last five percent of human existence. Archeology finds little evidence of weapons or war-gods or dominator societies before 4,000 B.C.E.

Myth: War is inevitable because of crises beyond our control like resource scarcity, environmental crises, over-population, etc.

Fact: humans are capable of rational behavior. War is always a choice and other choices are always possible if humans use their genetically endowed imaginations and inventiveness. Nonviolent resistance is always a choice, as are negotiation, economic sanctions, and many other responses to aggression.

Myth: We are a sovereign nation.

Fact: sovereignty rests on the belief that a people can draw a line around themselves and keep out anything they do not want to enter their nation, by war as a last resort. In fact, borders are now wholly permeable. One cannot keep out intercontinental ballistic missiles, ideas and information, disease organisms, refugees and migrants, economic influences, new technologies, the effects of climate shift, cyber-attacks, and cultural artifacts such as films and musical trends. Furthermore, most countries are not at all homogeneous but have highly mixed populations.

Myth: We go to war to ensure our defense.

Fact: "defense" is different from "offense." Defense means to protect one's borders from incursion as opposed to aggression, which is to cross another nation's borders to attack them. Establishing military bases around the world is offensive and it is counterproductive, stimulating hostility and threats rather than eliminating them. It makes us less secure. A defensive military posture would consist only of a coast guard, border patrol, anti-aircraft weapons, and other forces able to repel attack. Current "defense spending" by the U.S. Is almost wholly for projecting military power worldwide: offense, not defense.

> *"But if the term has any meaning, it cannot be stretched to cover offensive war making or aggressive militarism. If 'defense' is to mean something other than 'offense,' then attacking another nation 'so that they can't attack us first' or 'to send a message' or to 'punish' a crime is not defensive and not necessary."*
> - David Swanson (Author, Activist)

Myth: Some wars are "good" wars; for example, World War II.

Fact: it is true that cruel regimes were destroyed in World War 2, but to assert this is to use a curious definition of "good." World War 2 resulted in overwhelming destruction of cities and all their cultural treasures, in an economic loss of unprecedented proportions, in massive environmental pollution, and (not least) the deaths of 100 million people, the maiming and dislocation of millions of others, the birth of two new superpowers, and the unleashing of the age of nuclear terror. And both sides of World War 2 had the option in the preceding years and decades, of taking steps that would have avoided warfare.

Myth: the "Just War Doctrine"

Fact: the Doctrine of Just War, i.e., that a war is justified in spite of the general injunction to prefer peace, comes out of a fourth century C.E. rejection of the traditional Christian practice of pacifism. This doctrine stated that in order to go to war many criteria had to be satisfied, including that the war had to be fought with proportionate means (the evil of the destruction could not outweigh the evil of not going to war), and that civilians were never to be attacked. The purposeful slaughter of civilians by mass aerial bombardment and the onset of the colossal deadliness of nuclear weapons make world war ii an unjust war. In fact, given modern weapons (even so-called "smart bombs") it is impossible to wage war without killing innocent children, women, old men, and other non-combatants. Calling this evil "collateral damage" does not make an exception for it — it simply describes it with a deceitful euphemism. Finally, the now-proven alternative of nonviolent defense provides a resistance response to tyranny and invasion that satisfies all the criteria of just war without destroying millions of lives and is a response that returns civilization to original "Christian" values. No war can satisfy the conditions of absolute last resort. In the wars of the last twenty years, the most important motive has been to control the flow of oil out of the middle east, and, as we have seen, the so-called "war on terror" has only created more terrorists. However, a permanent state of war does benefit a small elite of war manufacturers and suppliers and serves as an excuse to restrict civil liberties.

Myth: War and war preparation bring peace and stability.

Fact: the ancient romans said, "if you want peace, prepare for war." What they got was war after war until it destroyed them. What the romans considered "peace" was dictating terms to the helpless conquered, much as occurred after World War 1 at which time an observer said that this was not a peace but a truce that would last only twenty years, which turned out to be the case. Making war creates resentment, new enemies, distrust, and further wars. Preparation for war makes other nations feel they must also prepare and so a vicious circle is created which perpetuates the war system.

Myth: War makes us safe. War may be unjust and bloody but in the end it makes us safe. Corollary: "The price of freedom is blood."

Fact: war makes everyone less safe. The losers lose, the winners lose, and all the survivors lose. In fact, no one wins a modern war. Many are killed on both sides. If by chance the "winners" fight the war in the losers' land, the winners nevertheless have many killed, spend treasure that could have been used to benefit their own citizens, and pollute the earth through greenhouse gas emissions and the release of toxins. The "victorious war" paves the way for future arms races and instability, leading eventually to the next war. War simply doesn't work.

Myth: War is necessary to kill the terrorists.

Fact: war mythology tells us that "our" wars (whoever "we" are) kill evil people who need to be killed to protect us and our freedoms. In fact, while some "terrorists" are killed, recent wars waged by wealthy nations are one-sided slaughters of innocents and ordinary residents and end up creating more terrorists while poisoning the natural environment. Rather than choosing a violent response to terrorism or invasion, which are just symptoms of a conflict problem, it is more sensible to look for the causes of the disease which has led to the conflict. In particular, it is more effective to learn about the history and what part your nation might have played in creating the conflict and the hostility so that the problem can be dealt with at its root. Otherwise, a violent response just perpetuates and escalates the conflict.

Myth: War is good for the economy and benefits the war makers.

Fact: war and war preparation weaken an economy. Some people argue that it was world war ii that got the west or the united states out of the great depression. In fact, it was government deficit spending that restarted the economy. The spending just happened to be on war production, things that when used nevertheless destroyed economic value. The spending could have gone for economic goods that improved the standard of living. It is well documented that a dollar spent on education and health care produces more jobs than the same dollar spent in the war industry, and a dollar spent on use value (rather than bombs) such as rebuilding roads or establishing green energy provides for the common good. Dollars spent to maintain the flow of oil end up polluting not only where it is eventually burned, but the oil used to power the military machine (in the U.S., 340,000 Barrels a day) also leads to a degrading of the environment. While war spending benefits a small number of war profiteers, peace is good for everyone and for the natural environment.

KELLOGG-BRIAND PACT 1928 (HANDOUT)

Treaty between the United States and other Powers providing for the renunciation of war as an instrument of national policy. Signed at Paris, August 27, 1928; ratification advised by the Senate, January 16, 1929; ratified by the President, January 17, 1929; instruments of ratification deposited at Washington by the United States of America, Australia, Dominion of Canada, Czechoslovkia, Germany, Great Britain, India, Irish Free State, Italy, New Zealand, and Union of South Africa, March 2, 1929: By Poland, March 26, 1929; by Belgium, March 27 1929; by France, April 22, 1929; by Japan, July 24, 1929; proclaimed, July 24, 1929.

BY THE PRESIDENT OF THE UNITED STATES OF AMERICA.
A PROCLAMATION.

WHEREAS a Treaty between the President of the United States Of America, the President of the German Reich, His Majesty the King of the Belgians, the President of the French Republic, His Majesty the King of Great Britain, Ireland and the British Dominions beyond the Seas, Emperor of India, His Majesty the King of Italy, His Majesty the Emperor of Japan, the President of the Republic of Poland, and the President of the Czechoslovak Republic, providing for the renunciation of war as an instrument of national policy, was concluded and signed by their respective Plenipotontiaries at Paris on the twenty-seventh day of August, one thousand nine hundred and twenty-eight, the original of which Treaty, being in the English and the French languages, is word for word as follows:

THE PRESIDENT OF THE GERMAN REICH, THE PRESIDENT OF THE UNITED STATES OF AMERICA, HIS MAJESTY THE KING OF THE BELGIANS, THE PRESIDENT OF THE FRENCH REPUBLIC, HIS MAJESTY THE KING OF GREAT BRITAIN IRELAND AND THE BRITISH DOMINIONS BEYOND THE SEAS, EMPEROR OF INDIA, HIS MAJESTY THE KING OF ITALY, HIS MAJESTY THE EMPEROR OF JAPAN, THE PRESIDENT OF THE REPUBLIC OF POLAND THE PRESIDENT OF THE CZECHOSLOVAK REPUBLIC,

Deeply sensible of their solemn duty to promote the welfare of mankind;

Persuaded that the time has, come when a frank renunciation of war as an instrument of na tional policy should be made to the end that the peaceful and friendly relations now existing between their peoples may be perpetuated;

Convinced that all changes in their relations with one another should be sought only by pacific means and be the result of a peaceful and orderly process, and that any signatory Power which shall hereafter seek to promote its ts national interests by resort to war a should be denied the benefits furnished by this Treaty;

Hopeful that, encouraged by their example, all the other nations of the world will join in this humane endeavor and by adhering to the present Treaty as soon as it comes into force bring their peoples within the scope of its beneficent provisions, thus uniting the civilized nations of the world in a common renunciation of war as an instrument of their national policy;

Have decided to conclude a Treaty and for that purpose have appointed as their respective

Plenipotentiaries:

THE PRESIDENT OF THE GERMAN REICH:
Dr Gustav STRESEMANN, Minister of Foreign Affairs;

THE PRESIDENT OF THE UNITED STATES OF AMERICA:
The Honorable Frank B. KELLOGG, Secretary of State;

HIS MAJESTY THE KING OF THE BELGIANS:
Mr Paul HYMANS, Minister for Foreign Affairs, Minister of State;

THE PRESIDENT OF THE FRENCH REPUBLIC:
Mr. Aristide BRIAND Minister for Foreign Affairs;

HIS MAJESTY THE KING OF GREAT BRITAIN, IRELAND AND THE BRITISH DOMINIONS BEYOND THE SEAS, EMPEROR OF INDIA:
For GREAT BRITAIN and NORTHERN IRELAND and all parts of the British Empire which are not separate

Members of the League of Nations:
The Right Honourable Lord CUSHENDUN, Chancellor of the Duchy of Lancaster, Acting-Secretary of State for Foreign Affairs;

For the DOMINION OF CANADA:
The Right Honourable William Lyon MACKENZIE KING, Prime Minister and Minister for External Affairs;

For the COMMONWEALTH of AUSTRALIA:
The Honourable Alexander John McLACHLAN, Member of the Executive Federal Council;

For the DOMINION OF NEW ZEALAND:
The Honourable Sir Christopher James PARR High Commissioner for New Zealand in Great Britain;

For the UNION OF SOUTH AFRICA:
The Honourable Jacobus Stephanus SMIT, High Commissioner for the Union of South Africa in Great Britain;

For the IRISH FREE STATE:
Mr. William Thomas COSGRAVE, President of the Executive Council;

For INDIA:
The Right Honourable Lord CUSHENDUN, Chancellor of the Duchy of Lancaster, Acting Secretary of State for Foreign Affairs;

HIS MAJESTY THE KING OF ITALY:
Count Gaetano MANZONI, his Ambassador Extraordinary and Plenipotentiary at Paris.

HIS MAJESTY THE EMPEROR OF JAPAN:
Count UCHIDA, Privy Councillor;

THE PRESIDENT OF THE REPUBLIC OF POLAND:
Mr. A. ZALESKI, Minister for Foreign Affairs;

THE PRESIDENT OF THE CZECHOSLOVAK REPUBLIC:
Dr Eduard BENES, Minister for Foreign Affairs;

who, having communicated to one another their full powers found in good and due form have agreed upon the following articles:

ARTICLE I

The High Contracting Parties solemnly declare in the names of their respective peoples that they condemn recourse to war for the solution of international controversies, and renounce it, as an instrument of national policy in their relations with one another.

ARTICLE II

The High Contracting Parties agree that the settlement or solution of all disputes or conflicts of whatever nature or of whatever origin they may be, which may arise among them, shall never be sought except by pacific means.

ARTICLE III

The present Treaty shall be ratified by the High Contracting Parties named in the Preamble in accordance with their respective constitutional requirements, and shall take effect as between them as soon as all their several instruments of ratification shall have been deposited at Washington.

This Treaty shall, when it has come into effect as prescribed in the preceding paragraph, remain open as long as may be necessary for adherence by all the other Powers of the world. Every instrument evidencing the adherence of a Power shall be deposited at Washington and the Treaty shall immediately upon such deposit become effective as; between the Power thus adhering and the other Powers parties hereto.

It shall be the duty of the Government of the United States to furnish each Government named in the Preamble and every Government subsequently adhering to this Treaty with a certified copy of the Treaty and of every instrument of ratification or adherence. It shall also be the duty of the Government of the United States telegraphically to notify such Governments immediately upon the deposit with it of each instrument of ratification or adherence.

IN FAITH WHEREOF the respective Plenipotentiaries have signed this Treaty in the French and English languages both texts having equal force, and hereunto affix their seals.

DONE at Paris, the twenty seventh day of August in the year one thousand nine hundred and twenty-eight.

[SEAL] GUSTAV STRESEMANN
[SEAL] FRANK B KELLOGG
[SEAL] PAUL HYMANS
[SEAL] ARI BRIAND

[SEAL] CUSHENDUN
[SEAL] W. L. MACKENZIE KING
[SEAL] A J MCLACHLAN
[SEAL] C. J. PARR
[SEAL] J S. SMIT
[SEAL] LIAM T.MACCOSGAIR
[SEAL] CUSHENDUN
[SEAL] G. MANZONI
[SEAL] UCHIDA
[SEAL] AUGUST ZALESKI
[SEAL] DR EDWARD BENES

Certified to be a true copy of the signed original deposited with the Government of the United States of America.

FRANK B. KELLOGG
Secretary of State of the United States of America

AND WHEREAS it is stipulated in the said Treaty that it shall take effect as between the High Contracting Parties as soon as all the several instruments of ratification shall have been deposited at Washington;

AND WHEREAS the said Treaty has been duly ratified on the parts of all the High Contracting Parties and their several instruments of ratification have been deposited with the Government of the United States of America, the last on July 24, 1929;

NOW TIIEREFORE, be it known that I, Herbert Hoover, President of the United States of America, have caused the said Treaty to be made public, to the end that the same and every article and clause thereof may be observed and fulfilled with good faith by the United States and the citizens thereof.

IN TESTIMONY WHEREOF, I have hereunto set my hand and caused the seal of the United States to be affixed.

DONE at the city of Washington this twenty-fourth day of July in the year of our Lord one thousand nine hundred and twenty-nine, and of the Independence of the United States of America the one hundred and fifty-fourth

HERBERT HOOVER
By the President:
HENRY L STIMSON
Secretary of State

NOTE BY THE DEPARTMENT OF STATE

ADHERING COUNTRIES

When this Treaty became effective on July 24, 1929, the instruments of ratification of all of the signatory powers having been deposited at Washington, the following countries, having deposited instruments of definitive adherence, became parties to it:

Afghanistan, Albania, Austria, Bulgaria, China, Cuba, Denmark, Dominican Republic, Egypt, Estonia, Ethiopia, Finland, Guatemala, Hungary, Iceland, Latvia, Liberia, Lithuania, Netherlands, Nicaragua, Norway, Panama, Peru, Portugal, Rumania, Russia, Kingdom of the Serbs, Croats and Slovenes, Siam, Spain, Sweden, Turkey

Additional adhesions deposited subsequent to July 24, 1929. Persia, July 2, 1929; Greece, August 3, 1929; Honduras, August 6, 1929; Chile, August 12, 1929; Luxemburg August 14, 1929; Danzig, September 11, 1929; Costa Rica, October 1, 1929; Venezuela, October 24, 1929.

Source:
United States Statutes at Large
Vol 46 Part 2 Page 2343